BEAR AND MOOSE

The Saga of Big Game Hunting in the Northeast Wilderness

Norm Jolliffe

North Country Press · Thorndike, Maine

Library of Congress Cataloging-in-Publication Data:

Jolliffe, Norm.
  Bear & moose.

   1. Bear hunting — Northeastern States.   2. Moose
hunting — Northeastern States.   3. Bears — Northeastern
States.   4. Moose — Northeastern States.   5. Mammals —
Northeastern States.   I. Title.   II. Title: Bear and moose.
SK295.J65   1987   799.2'774446   87-24853
ISBN 0-89621-111-8 *MT 110*

L.L. Bean   8.95   12-94

Cover design by James B. Murray.

To Anita,
who unabashed has
ministered lovingly to the author
for much longer than he has tended
to this production

PROLOGUE

---

*"You don't want to lose game you plan to kill
because your rifle doesn't work"*
—the Hermit of Blackfly Lake, in conversation, 10/11/86.

MY editor and I have agreed that I am to write a prologue to this bear and moose book, and that I am to write something as an epilogue, also. "A book should be like a sandwich," he has said.

Of course, the first thought in mind is an apology to all the gun hunters that will be reading this opus. Although I pick up rifles now and then for hunting purposes, or feel an obligation to fondle and inspect firearms of friends and other hunters, I feel stronger emotions toward bows and arrows.

I own several 7mm rifles—but my preference for that specific numerical measurement of bullet size (7mm-08, 7 X 57, 7mm-06, and 7mm Magnum) is because I think seven is a lucky number. Quite frankly I can discern no other reason.

I also own seven cats. Six of these are functional and one is merely decorative. Of the working cats, the most vicious is contained in a latched box. It accompanies me to my hunting camp when I go there. It is used for mouse control. When not working at the camp this cat patrols my office in my home stalking mice. On occasion it brings to bay trespassing wild animals much larger than itself. The other five working cats are outside creatures basically living for their own purposes, working to support themselves by harvesting songbirds. Oh, the seventh cat is one that has been taxidermied to fit inside a knitting basket. Cunning!

I had this 300 Winchester Magnum once, when I lived in Alaska, and I was considering one time firing it at a grizzly that happened to be inspecting me at the short distance of only 30 yards. I considered and the grizzly considered, and lucky for us both the grizzly backed off. He wasn't fully prime anyway. My hands were shaking when I tried to remove the cartridge from my rifle, and the clip extractor broke, leaving the loaded round stuck in the chamber. So what I had, really, was a single-shot rifle. I could have fired that round at the grizzly, but probably the extractor would have broke, and I would have had no way to get off a second shot fast enough. The bear would have been only wounded and I would have been dead. Unlike a black bear, a grizzly doesn't die with just one bullet in him. Anyway, the point is I shouldn't have been using that 300 Winchester Magnum on any kind of big game, dangerous or docile. A hunter needs a rifle that will function each time, no exceptions, every time he uses it, under a variety of conditions—hot or cold, blowing sand or snow or salt water. You don't want to lose game you plan to kill because your rifle doesn't work.

The best, most reliable kind of action is the bolt-action. Autos are very fast but the ammo for them has to be perfect. I'll bet that anyone who has a favorite auto has had it jam on him at least a dozen times in the field. Pumps and levers are faster than bolts, but they are not as strong or as accurate. Besides, with practice, most hunters can shoot bolts just as fast or even faster than they can pumps and levers.

Of course, there are bolts and there are bolts. Remingtons are especially accurate. Winchesters are smooth. My 300 Magnum was smooth, at least. Rugers are made well. But the actions designed to be rugged—reliable—are the military designs. These include Mausers, Springfields, and Enfields. Ask those fancy custom gunsmiths in New York, Mat Griffin and George Howe, the kind of bolt action they prefer a customer to choose when they build a $10,000 rifle for him. That would be one with a full-claw extractor, positive ejector, and strong firing-pin fall. It would also be one with a slight looseness when the bolt is operated, which is good, because that means dirt, dust, sand and ice aren't going to bother it. You want that rifle to shoot when you climb a messy mountain in Mongolia to tag a goat that costs $20,000. In any case, I prefer Mauser actions. Specifically I prefer the 98-Mauser as the most reliable and safest action ever devised.

Triggers. A trigger should be good and crisp to shoot the rifle accurately. Adjustable triggers are okay. But for dangerous game—and I don't know if I would put black bear and moose in that category—what you have to do is shoot him dead off his feet at ten yards when he's charging. So you want a simple, rugged trigger that's not so crisp and nicely accurate. In that kind of nervous situation a hunter will jerk the trigger, not squeeze it with deliberate slowness. A simple, rugged trigger won't fail you in that situation, and you can't fail it.

Barrels. Twenty to twenty-four inches is right for everyone. If you're not up to keeping your barrel oiled regularly, then you might want to have a stainless steel barrel. Another advantage of stainless is because you don't oil it you don't have an oil scent to worry about that might spook big game.

Stocks. Synthetic stocks are as ugly as hell, but extremely tough and contributory to accuracy. Synthetics don't need oil either. Wood stocks should at least be glass-bedded and the barrel free-floated. I was guiding in the days before synthetic stocks, but back then I always told my clients about glass-bedding and free-floating as accuracy-improvers. These days synthetic stocks do that job much better.

Sights. Scopes are best. A quality, light, $2^{1}/_{2}$ fixed-power is excellent and best for big game at 300 yards or 30 feet. Actually any fixed-power between $2^{1}/_{2}$ to 4 is going to be okay. But $2^{1}/_{2}$ is optimum, I think. Those big variables are too heavy. I have a 2 to 7 power on my 7mm Magnum. Variables are not as reliable as fixed magnification scopes. They fog up much more frequently than the fixed. Iron sights are useful in fog or rain. The reliable hunting rifle should have iron sights, too. I may add that the iron sights should be sighted in for a standard factory ammo available in remote regions. Of course that should be the same ammo you're shooting with the scope.

Caliber. With caliber as with the rifle components I've been discussing, the prime consideration is practicality and versatility. The caliber has to be powerful enough for all the big game you want to hunt. There should be the widest possible bullet selection. The recoil should be tolerable. And factory ammo for it has to be available in remote regions. Of course, I'm talking 30-06. It will work on anything. The 30-06 has the highest percentage of kills per shots fired than any other caliber. The 270 has the next highest. The big magnums are not necessary. Besides, most hunters can't shoot them well enough.

The shiny rifle. No, you don't want the rifle shiny. Polished surfaces that look good in a showroom or in the

gun rack of your trophy room have the bad habit of spook-
ing big game almost as fast as their noses in your arm pits.
All exposed metal finishes should be dulled. You can do that
with black electrical tape or flat-black Rustoleum stove
paint.

A sling. The rifle should have one. Detachable swivels
sometimes detach by themselves. So permanent swivels are
better. By better I mean more reliable, of course.

For the perfect rifle, sonny, you'll have to go to a custom gunsmith. Or you may have to visit several custom
gunsmiths along the way. But what you want is 30-06 caliber, a stainless steel barrel 24 inches long, a Mauser bolt
action, a synthetic stock especially fitted to you, a compact
2¹/₂ power scope, iron sights, a sling that won't come off
accidentally, no shiny metal, and a crisp trigger. Good bullets for it would be 150, 165 or 180-grain. That rifle may
prefer one weight over the others, but any bullet in that
weight-category would work well on black bear and moose.

PART 1

NORTHEASTERN BEAR

CHAPTER 1

*Appreciation of the black bear in the past depended on
who you were—the native American with rooted traditions
and values or the colonial white with fears.*

BLACK bear, moose, deer, and probably caribou were the
favorite foods of almost all the precolonial Indian tribes
inhabiting what we call now (at least for purposes of this
book) the Northeast Wilderness. Pumpkins, corn, and
beans were reliable and filling and necessary as a dietary
balance, but big-game meats were considered tastier.
Present-day Indians I have spoken with—Passamaquoddies
living in Princeton and Penobscots living in Old Town,
Maine—generally rate moose as best, deer second, and bear
last. They know nothing of caribou. (The cause of the
woodland caribou demise in modern Maine, New York,
New Brunswick and Nova Scotia is complex—but is basically due to the destruction by lumbering of the lichen
ranges and old growth timber, harboring tree lichens, and
the introduction into these cut-over areas of a competing
species, the whitetail deer.)

"Moose, deer, and bear—in that order," Russell Roy, a
Penobscot forester, told me. "It's close between moose and
deer. Moose tastes more like beef than deer, and you don't
have to cook it as hard. Bear is way on the bottom of my

list. Bear tends to be tough and greasy. I prefer beef and pork to bear."

Appreciation by some still goes beyond mere palatability, however. The fact that the bear is the animal which in physical structure most resembles the human form must have been considered seriously by the Indians: a skinned bear very much resembles a skinned man.

"On a one to ten scale, I'd rate bear a ten," David Tomah, a Passamaquoddy game warden stated. "Moose would be nine or so and deer two or three. Beef and pork rate five or six. I like moose steak the best. Bear I wouldn't shoot because I still believe in the old ways. I might trap one, but I don't know. If I had a chance, I wouldn't eat bear meat, because bear are sacred to me. . . . Other Passamaquoddies feel this way. Some don't. Don't know about the Penobscots."

The oldest Indian deities are the animals, and the myths and legends speak of various animals as the progenitors of the tribes—a specimen of some animal having been at one time transformed into a human ancestor. As I understand it, the Passamaquoddy belief is that they are descended from a black bear. Hence the black bear is their totum, and if not now sacred to all tribal members, at least respected by many and hunted with ceremony or not considered fair game.

Indians worshipped nature—not only animals, but also meadows, streams, mountains, the wind, individual trees and specific rocks. Everytime an Indian did something important—such as hunting game or planting corn—the act was done with ritual and prayer.

Smoking was a religious act. Northern Indians, of course, couldn't raise tobacco, so they smoked substitutes. Bearberry bark mixed with bearberry leaves was one such substitute. The bearberry is a trailing shrub with small ever-green leaves and red berries. I have tried this bearberry to-bacco—"kinnikinnick"—in my pipe and must admit that I didn't enjoy it. Ceremony—not enjoyment—was the main purpose, however. I suppose that bears eat bearberry berries. Though bears must prefer strawberries and raspberries.

The precolonials rarely hunted big game for sport. I have a book, THE GOSPEL OF THE REDMAN, put together by Ernest and Julia Seton and given to me and autographed by Mrs. Seton in 1948 when she found me on her doorstep in New Mexico dehydrated and hungry. I was biking from California to New York and she must have thought I was in need of some faith as well as orange juice. Anyway, the book contains a poem, of not-exactly-speci-fied authorship, titled TO A DEAD DEER.

"I am sorry I had to kill thee, Little brother.
But I had need of thy meat.
My children were hungry and crying for food.
Forgive me, Little Brother.
I will do honour to thy courage, thy strength and
    thy beauty.
See, I will hang thy horns on this tree.
I will decorate them with red streamers.
Each time I pass, I will remember thee and do honour
    to thy spirit.
I am sorry I had to kill thee.
Forgive me, Little Brother.
See, I smoke to thy memory.
I burn tobacco."

This poem is both romanticism and truth. There is a preponderance of the romantic, but the point is valid that

Indians rarely hunted for sport. That doesn't mean, however, they didn't have fun when they hunted—the kind of
fun roughly parallel to chasing down a barnyard rooster for
Sunday dinner or catching the pig to kill him for scalding
and shaving.

   This is not really fun with a capital F, of course. But
there is certainly exercise involved, agility is necessary, and
the end result is a certain exhilaration and a kind of pleasure.
So Indians when they hunted must have felt the rush of
adrenalin, thumping hearts, and their hands must have
shaken just a little, at least. The Indians were involved in
agricultural hunting, not sport hunting. Although hunting
involved the same weapons as war (club, spear, and bow
and arrow) hunting was not nearly as glamourous. War was
the captivation. The Indians delighted in creeping to villages
of rival tribes, attacking with shouts, killing and capturing,
or frequently merely touching their foes. There are few rules
and regulations in agricultural hunting. Mostly you do
whatever you have to do to get the job done. In sport
hunting rules and regulations are imposed to make the taking of game difficult—either to measure the skill of the
hunter or to conserve animals or both. The rules and ethics
of modern sport-hunting are close to the same conventions
of good taste as a precolonial Indian-vs-Indian war.

   Hunting—and trapping—were essential occupations
of the precolonial Indians. Perhaps hunting and trapping
were more important later when trading with whites became possible. Today hunting and trapping are regarded by
Indians as traditional rights with unique privileges, but not
as essential occupations.

   Tribes in the lower areas of the Northeast Wilderness
spent more time raising vegetables than tribes farther north.

But all the Indians would eat almost all the animals they took by hunting and trapping—and the deer species and "tough and greasy" black bear were their favorite foods.

Indian agricultural hunting was highly organized. They knew the territories they hunted intimately and where the animals were located and when the animals would be there for the required seasonal catch. Hunts were often like roundups: in the case of deer, for example, large numbers were surrounded and driven into corrals where they could be slaughtered and butchered conveniently. The Indians would concentrate on one species at a time—not killing a bear, for example, when it was the season for hunting deer. They also treated game as a renewable resource—dividing hunting territories into tracts and hunting the tracts in rotation over the years.

Indians hunted bears in the winter—"the season when the elk and deer are lean." The hunting tract was carefully examined for dens and dens located—by obviously following tracks in the snow and looking for claw marks on trees or by deftly locating the breathing holes of dens on frosty, still mornings, when even slight exhalations would freeze and hang in the heavy air. Bear were forced out of the dens and killed with bows and arrows, or killed inside the dens with spears, or sometimes a hunter would enter a den and club a bear to "knock out his brains before he can open his eyes," according to one colonial white account. This must have been an exceptional occurance, however, because bear dens are extremely confining.

In the spring bears were trapped in deadfalls, according to another account. "A log was placed on the ground in a place frequented by the game. Near the large end of the tree two stakes of the proper size and length were driven into the earth, one on each side, to keep it in its place. Directly over this another tree was placed, with the top or small end suspended to a proper height betwixt the stakes, by the usual contrivance of the figure 4, or by a small cord connected with a spindle. Upon the spindle bait was placed and if the slightest nibble was made at the bait, the curious intruder was secured by the fall of the suspended tree."

Tanned and dressed bear hides were used as bedding, as a medium of exchange among the tribes, and as clothing: "Mantles made of bear skins is a usual wearing among the natives that live where the bears do haunt. Where the men use but one bear skin for a mantle, the women have two sewed together."

Bear flesh was esteemed as juicy and well-flavored. Frequently a whole bear was roasted at feasts. At these ceremonies there were no leftovers—the entire bear was consumed, including the paws and the grease, which was drunk. On lesser occasions, however, bear grease was retained to be used later as a basting on turkey or for medicinal, cosmetic, and ornamental purposes. For example, Canadian Indians anointed themselves "when they are excessively cold, tired with labor, hurt, and in other cases. They believe it softens the skin, and makes the body pliant, and is very serviceable to old age." And, also, one Indian cure for earache was "bear gall"—extracted from a freshly killed animal, then dried, powdered, dissolved in water, and dropped into the suffering aural cavity.

At least 11,000 years ago Indians inhabited the Northeast Wilderness. Archeologists have discovered knives and scrapers and other artifacts among the remains of caribou, about 11,000 years old, at a site of early hunters in Nova Scotia and at another such site in Michigan. It is assumed that these Northeast Indians killed mastadons, musk ox, giant beaver and elk, and moose and bear.

The bow and arrow came into use as a hunting and war weapon somewhere between 500 B.C. and 500 A.D. It was either discovered or introduced. If it was introduced, this was probably accomplished by Vikings. Before the bow, however, the atlatl was used. The atlatl is a spear-throwing device that is very old, having been used in Asia and Europe and America for thousands of years before the advent of the bow. Basically the atlatl is a stick with one knob end (where you hold it) and one hook end. The spear fits into the hook end. By precisely drilling a small, smoothed stone and fitting it over the atlatl, thereby giving it more weight, the atlatl becomes an effective, efficient tool for launching a spear. The spear shaft is held in place by the hunter's thumb and forefinger. The atlatl helps throw a spear with more accuracy and greater force than normally possible using just the leverage of the arm alone.

Three types of bows were used by North American Indians: the self bow made from one piece of wood and dependent entirely upon the elasticity of its wooden arms; the reinforced bow, also of one piece of wood, but with its back lined with cast-improving sinew; and the composite bow—sinew on the back and horn on the belly—developed out west around 1700. The composite bow was considerably shorter than the self bow and was convenient for shooting while riding a horse. The reinforced bow outperformed the self bow. The composite bow outperformed them both. In hunting situations, the Indians preferred bows and arrows over firearms. Bows were quieter and didn't spook game nearly as much. Also Indians could reload and shoot bows faster than they could muzzleloading firearms. When hunt-

ing conditions changed and firearms improved, Indians preferred rifles over bows.

The self bow was the only type of bow ever used by
Indians of the Northeast Wilderness. The English longbow
is a self bow—and generally much better in design than
Indian self bows. The so-called Sudbury bow is one of the
better examples of Indian self-bow design and workman-
ship. It is on exhibit at the Peabody Museum of Harvard
University. A faded inscription, written in ink on the belly,
says: ". . . taken from an Indian in Sudbury, Mass., A.D.
1660, by William Goodnough who shot the Indian while he
was ransacking the Goodnough house for plunder . . . . "

The Sudbury bow, about 67 inches long, is made from
hickory and expertly tillered. Saxton Pope, the noted
archery historian and anthropologist, in 1920 made an exact
copy of this bow from a dense-grained, well-seasoned stave
of red hickory. The Sudbury copy had a pull-weight of 46
pounds at 28 inches and could shoot a hunting arrow 173
yards. Pope said of the replica: "It is soft and pleasant to
shoot, and could do effective work either as a hunting or a
war implement."

The white man's fur trade thoroughly ruined the cul-
tures of the Northeast Indians. When the animals were gone
that had provided the furs, white settlers moved in, forcing
treaties upon the Indians to get their lands. Since the Indians
were economically (and culturally) powerless by this time,
about 1815, they either emigrated out west, where some
tribes retained dignity for some years, or they remained
where they were to live in situations of extreme deprivation.
The Indian-white engagement had been an insidious economic and cultural war—with periods of physical con-
flict—which the Indians lost.

CHAPTER 2

The colonial white's fears from the past into the present.

THE colonial whites converted much of the land from—as a contemporary historian said, in 1653—something that was "remote, rocky, barren, bushy, wild-woody wilderness [into] a second England for fertileness."

Henry David Thoreau noted that by 1855 there was a certain loss. Bear and moose headed his list of what was mostly gone, along with deer, porcupines, the wolf, beaver, marten, bass, alewives, eagles, pigeons, turkeys, etc. "I cannot but feel," Thoreau wrote, "as if I lived in a tamed, and, as it were, emasculated country."

The bear was diminished and wolves were exterminated because both species were regarded (with fears that were mostly justified) as property destroyers. The deer, moose and caribou were greatly reduced in numbers because the intense agriculture practiced by the newcomers severely degraded the quality of their habitats. Also, these deer species were overhunted.

The habit bears have of congregating in areas of seasonably abundant food—for example, ripening oat and blueberry fields in the summer or wherever sucker and salmon runs are occuring in the spring—tended to concern the colonials: "In September [1663] there came very many bears out of the wilderness, so that several hundreds were killed of them by the English in several parts of colony." And in 1699: "A strange descent of hundreds of bears, infesting the road I was to travel, alarmed all people, but I met none of them."

It didn't take bruin long to realize that the new agriculture being energetically practiced by the colonials represented his opportunity to grab food. Bears ate, on occasion, sheep and pigs. That is a developed habit bears still enjoy.

The whites hunted bears as did the Indians—by finding the winter dens and forcing the occupants out with fire. When an aggravated bruin eventually emerged he would be greeted by bullets from unwieldly match-locks and wheel-locks. (Arrows discharged from longbows would have been more efficient!) The whites also hunted bears with dogs, which the Indians had never done: "The object of the hunter is to compel [the bear] to take to a tree. This [the bear] is disposed to do when the dog bites him . . . or annoys him with a continual bark." The English introduced the hound into America. The typical Indian dog was a barking garbage eater, not a hunting dog. The Indians raised their dogs as domestic livestock to be consumed when desirable or necessary much as the whites raised pigs and cattle.

The whites, again like the Indians, practiced circle drives—surrounding and eventually concentrating bears and other wild animals into a particular area where all could be easily harvested. In addition the colonials evidently set out live bears—but much more frequently, live turkeys—at shooting contests: "where all gentlemen and others that would divert themselves may repair."

The circle drive as a hunting method has long been practiced in Europe. It is a reliable technique of agricultural hunting still legally used in parts of America today: in forests and brushlands, shouting men or barking dogs drive deer toward hidden hunters with rifles. It is the same as roundups into corrals or frightening buffaloes into plunging off a cliff.

Bear hunting was not a novelty to the colonials. They were well aware of the old traditions. Bears (a species of brown, of course—not black) were extremely common in the European forests of antiquity. Hunting them with dogs and spears was regarded as sport-hunting. Indeed, this must have been the case. Hunting bears with beaters, net-holders, and spears was also considered heroic. The net-holders had to be lively on their feet. The European brown bear was never considered blue-blooded game. Bruin was an out-lawed animal, as in the white colonies of America, because he was a property destroyer.

The abundance of bears was a problem in large areas of Europe during the Middle Ages. Many villages, at peasant expense, maintained packs of bear-hounds. But whenever a kill occured, the trophy and the coveted fat of the bear went to the ruling prince. The peasants consumed the meat. Those were the rules.

In the 1600s the brown bear became uncommon in European farm country except in Scandinavia and parts of Russia. The Swedes enjoyed themselves with their bear problem well into the 1800s. "Never retreat a single step from a bear with which you have come to grips," advised Hans Orre, a famous Swedish hunter. Orre, and others like him, practiced interesting techniques. One was to have the left arm (provided you were right-handed) swathed in thick rags or the left arm covered with metal plates studded with spikes. While the bear was busy chewing into the rags or the plates, it could be speared with the right arm. That was the theory. Bear were also shot from platforms erected over baits and at sets with crossbow and broadhead arrow. At sets the crossbow was secured to a tree stump and a string was tied from the trigger to well-positioned bait in a cubby. The Swedes also used deadfalls, jaw-traps, and circle drives. Like the Indians and colonials in America, the Swedes commonly hunted bears when they were in their winter dens. Although firearms were undoubtedly useful, spearing seems to have been the preferred bear-killing method even into the mid-nineteenth century. When bruin charged from his den, Sven wedged the rear end of his spear into the ground. When bruin attacked, he was impaled on the front end of the spear. Again, that was the theory. In any case, champion Swedish bear hunters claim thirty to forty bears in their lifetimes. One Finnish bear hunter, however, active in the late eighteenth century, documented a lifetime kill of 193 large bears—many taken using spearing techniques, I presume.

The colonials, like the Indians and the Swedes, found bear meat delicious. Probably licking his chops, one colonial wrote: "All who have tasted the flesh of this animal say that it is most delicious eating; a young bear, fattened with autumnal fruits, is a dish fit for the nicest epicure. It is wholesome and nourishing, and resembles pork more than any other meat." Another enthusiast reported that if the flesh of bears were prepared like ham, the result made "extraordinary" bacon. Another said: "Their flesh is eaten by both rich and poor, since it is equal in goodness to pork. The people are used to catch and kill them, and to use them instead of hogs."

The fat was honored more than the flesh. Pure white, the color of modern shortenings made from hydrogenated soybean and palm oils, bear fat may be rendered into a sweet, light oil. The colonials used bear oil for frying, baking and—according to one 1784 account—"sometimes use it instead of butter, or oil for salad." Another declared that bear oil was "a well-known popular remedy against baldness." And a doctor, writing in 1833, proclaimed the medical benefits of lard made from bear fat: "One Mr. Purchase cured himself of the sciatica with bears-grease, keeping some of it continually in his groin. It is good too for swelled cheeks upon cold, for rupture of the hands in winter, for limbs taken suddenly with sciatica, gout, [and] other diseases. . . ."

Early in the white colonial experience, because woven cloth was generally scarce and/or expensive, bearskins were widely used for bedding. And bearskin robes were valued by travelers: "These robes wear much longer than those of the buffalo, being in texture much stronger, and more impervious to rain; and, besides, they are considered much handsomer and richer in appearance."

The black bear population had declined greatly by the nineteenth century in much of the Northeast Wilderness— certainly near populated urban centers and in areas where agriculture was the dominant economic activity. In fact, wilderness in the northeast had diminished greatly. Vast areas of northern New England and New York, eastern Ontario, Quebec, and the Maritime Provinces were fence-to-fence farms. The wilderness in these areas had been "emasculated," to use Thoreau's term.

The advent of an occasional wandering black bear into a domesticated neighborhood was cause for consternation and alarm, as noted in one 1857 report: ". . .One morning saw a bear under the tree near the house. . . . Called the nearest neighbors, who came with their guns and dogs. The latter at once attacked the bear, who retreated across the land to the marsh below it and to the salt water—the men being unable to fire at him without endangering the dogs. He was driven into the bay, the dogs not following him further. The bear was now fired upon and wounded, and with difficulty reached the opposite shore. The men were soon upon the spot, and found him nearly exhausted with loss of blood; he was easily despatched, and the carcass carried home in triumph."

Manly Hardy, a noted field naturalist active in Maine at the same time Ernest Seton was active out west and in Canada, wrote in 1897: "The bear of today can only in rare instances be caught in the same way in which he could fifty years ago in places where he has been trapped. For many years he has known enough to tear down the sides of the house around the steel trap, and in some cases to take hold of the clay and haul the trap out of the house. A bear which is well educated can discount any wolf ever born in the tricks he can teach a trapper. Many can now be taken only by setting the traps in water with scent, as is practiced in setting for foxes."

By the 1900s bear and moose had retreated into the most remote corners of the Northeast Wilderness. Generally bear could not survive on the agricultural fringes as well as deer. Bruin, at least, survived by being perhaps more clever than his great-great-great-grandfather. Moose survived for other reasons that I will touch on later.

The gradual abandonment of farmland late into this century certainly makes it possible for the black bear to reestablish habitat. The Vikings arrived and retreated, quite likely (as mentioned before) leaving the Indians with the idea of the bow and arrow. The white colonials arrived, taking the Indian's land and the black bear's habitat. The average person of today (certainly the average writer of today is not like Henry David Thoreau) quite likely struggles with facts and figures displayed on a computer monitor, while the pines and maples spring to life in the "emasculated" hayfields so laboriously tended for three hundred years previously.

Maine is where I live and work—as a writer and outfitter—and of course Maine is that portion of the Northeast Wilderness with which I am most familiar. The black bear was once regarded as a nuisance species here. There was a bounty on bruin until 1969, when a limit of one per year per hunter was established.

The population in the 1950s was estimated at about 5000. In the 1970s the population was estimated at about 7500. Today, as I am writing this, the black bear population is put at approximately 18,000 specimens. Of course, probably the population-estimators had been wrong previously. Or were they right?

Of the 33,000 square miles in Maine some 23,000 are considered suitable black bear habitat. Today Maine has more habitat more suited to black bear than any other state in the northeastern U.S. So naturally Maine has a good number of black bear. I asked the Hermit of Blackfly Lake, a downeast personage of note whom I frequently consult regarding statistics, what he thought the population estimate should be.

"Bear are so thick at the dump this year they've hired a supervisor," the Hermit answered me, nibbling a garlic clove.

"You mean the hippy with the sunglasses?"

"No," the Hermit said, exhaling. "I mean the big bear with the armband."

CHAPTER 3

There is little information on record about the habits and habitat of the black bear.

LITTLE is known about the black bear—scientists are making discoveries, however. And the edibility of its flesh is a subject for argument. Deer meat is universally accepted by people, plus their dogs and cats. Bear meat . . . well . . . is marginally accepted. Compared with other bears, however, the meat of the black bear is the tastiest—but an Eskimo might argue otherwise, as might a Viking of 1000 A.D. The Vikings of Norway and Iceland relished boiled polar bear meat. Actually I have never tasted polar, or brown, or grizzly bear meat, so when I say black bear meat is the tastiest I am making a speculation based on mystical intuition, which means my speculation is unreasonable, even though possibly correct. But not enough is known about the black bear.

Ursus americanus has not been studied as methodically by qualified scientists as has, for example, *Odocoileus virginianus*. Black bear fans are not nearly as numerous as whitetail deer enthusiasts—that's one big reason. The other big reason is the reclusive nature of the black bear. It does not choose to make itself available to be studied methodically.

The meat of the black bear is coarse and darker than beef. It is not more coarse, however, than chuck portions of beef. The meat of an old black bear is generally tougher than the meat of a young one. The meat of an old black bear killed just out of hibernation is more tender than the meat of the same old black bear killed in October or November—a statement that is difficult to prove scientifically, yet not impossible to prove haphazardly. But it is impossible to kill the same old bear in the spring and then again in the fall. The solution to the problem requires imagination, of course, but the technology is there: tranquilize a bear in the spring, surgically remove a small portion of one ham; place a radio collar on the bear; find and tranquilize the bear in the fall, surgically remove another small portion of the same ham— then taste and compare. (Oh, yes. Don't forget to take the collar off the bear; and then to release the poor beast.) Such a procedure would be science-fiction, sadistic, impermissible—therefore unlikely ever to occur.

To determine the age of any bear one of its teeth (a premolar is best to work with) must be examined in a laboratory. The process involves putting the tooth in some formic acid to decalcify it and make it soft. Then the tooth is soaked in water to clean it, and frozen. The frozen tooth is then cut into sections with a cryostatic microtome and the sections stained. Five or six of the sections are then placed on a slide and viewed through a microscope. For each year that a bear lives a new layer of cementum is added to the old layers of cementum covering the roots of its teeth. By viewing the five or six stained sections of one premolar through a microscope these layers can be examined and counted. With very young bears the cementum layers are easy to see, but with really old bears the layers tend to merge together and are difficult to differentiate.

It is not uncommon for a biologist to count sixteen

cementum layers. That would be an old bear, or a decently mature bear, of about sixteen years. It is usual to count two or three layers. Most bear, like deer, are killed when they are rather young.

In 1974, in New York State, a large, vigorous, black bear was killed and his age determined by counting his cementum layers. They counted forty-two layers. I wouldn't be surprised (mystical intuition) if the hunter who killed the bear, when he had dressed his trophy and examined it, had estimated its age as fourteen to eighteen.

Not every bear that is killed has its cementum layers counted. Not every bear killed is considered a trophy either. The best black bear any of my hunters ever killed measured by the Boone and Crockett system (length of skull plus width of skull measured linearly) was $19^{11}/_{16}$ inches. That was a bear killed according to the rules of fair chase by an archer. The bear weighed 340 pounds. Once with a recurve bow I killed a bear that measured $18^{13}/_{16}$ inches. It weighed 450 pounds. Some years ago a woman hunting with the hounds of a Maine outfitter killed with a rifle a bear that weighed 525 pounds and measured $18^{12}/_{16}$ inches. About that same year, also, a man killed a bear that was gallompf-ing around his children's swing set. The man fired his rifle from inside his house. The bullet went through the window-glass first before killing the bear. This bear weighed 460 pounds and measured 21 inches.

The relatively ancient New York State bear was shot in Newcomb. It was a male. The skull measures about $20^1/_2$ inches. One of the canines in broken. The other three canines are worn down to $1/_2$ inch from the gum line. The molars also show considerable wear. The next oldest bear that they know about in New York State was also shot in

New York State. It had 33 cementum layers. It was shot in 1958.

There is a theory that the above bear might be a dump bear, and counting cementum layers in the premolar of a dump bear is not a reliable method of estimating its age. This is because a dump bear's eating habits at his pile of garbage are abnormal, and may cause him to grow extra cementum layers in particular years. But according to biologists employed by New York State some kind of stress is the only way a "false" cementum layer can be induced—and any "false" cementum layer can be identified as such. To their knowledge, "true" cementum layers are induced by photoperiodism—the relative exposure of an organism to daylight as a proportion of the total day—not nutrition. All mammalian teeth, including the teeth of non-hibernating species, have cementum layers corresponding to calendar years. They told me if I wanted to I could pull one of my teeth and send it to them, they could determine my age exactly.

In any case, if a bear has a big skull it might be old, or sixteen, or six. A bear weighing 300 pounds in the spring will weigh 450 pounds in the fall. The gain is mostly fatweight the bear will lose, not during the winter as you might suppose, but early in the spring. Of course its skull will become slightly larger each summer—and that does not shrink in the winter. Eastern black bear have smaller skulls than western black bear—that is to say, the vast majority of the Boone and Crockett trophies come out of the west. So then it may be said that the average eastern black bear when it is six will have a smaller skull than the average western specimen when it is six. Anyway, hunters talk about the western "race" of black bear as objects more worthy of chasing.

Ernest Seton in LIVES OF GAME ANIMALS (a work of several volumes published in 1909 and 1926 and still authoritative) writes: "Black bears may be red, white, blue, black, brown, yellow, silver, or gold. . . . As one nears the Mississippi, various shades of cinnamon brown are found, and in the Rocky Mountains, the browns increase. M.P. Skinner assures me that in Yellowstone Park, only half the bears are black. The difference of color, however, does not mean a difference of species; they are mere freaks or sports of the black race. A black bear may have cinnamon young this year, and black the next, or even one of each kind in the same litter. So also a cinnamon mother may give birth to either black or cinnamon young."

Although Seton observed far more specimens of western black bear than eastern, his conclusions apply generally, of course.

On sociability and voice: "The black bear is essentially a solitary animal. Occasionally a number of them have been seen together, but these gatherings were either for the purpose of mating, or were a family of grown-up young ones with their mother. Nine out of ten adult bears will be found leading solitary lives. . . . The black bear has a long list of vocal sounds to express his feelings to others of its kind. Besides the growl of anger and loud cough of menace, it has whining calls, and sniffs of many sorts, also a number of bawls expressing rage or pain."

On bear trees: "I have seen hundreds of . . . bear trees, chiefly in the Rocky Mountains. They are always by some well-worn pathway or trail of the bears, and are made and used by bears of all species. . . . It is very certain that such a remarkable and universal bear habit must have some good object. I think there can be no doubt . . . that these are . . .

methods of communicating certain information to (other) bears. They answer, I believe, the same purpose as the urinary signal posts of dogs, wolves, and foxes."

I have studied bear trees, too. A male bear will mark his territory and indicate how big and strong he is by standing on his hind legs and biting a chunk out of a tree he has in some particular manner selected. He will mark the same tree several years running—until quite often the tree is girdled and dies or until a hunter discovers the tree and ambushes the bear. In any case, a black bear is not strongly territorial. But he is territorial when there is a particular food, rather tasty, in his range and he wants to eat it all himself. A dead moose, for example, if bruin is able, he will covet and protect for himself. When a bear has a fight with another bear the occasion is serious. They roar, snarl, growl, click teeth, claw and bite, wrestle and slap. Other bears do not sit around watching the performance or listening—they leave quickly to wherever they can't see or hear the racket.

Seton on the black bear as tree-climber: "I shall never forget the surprise I got when first I saw a wild one climb a tree. I had pictured to myself something like the slow moving up of a man or a sloth, or at best, the action of an expert sailor going up the shrouds. But what I really saw was more like the action of a cat. It had not the spring and agility of a squirrel or marten, but this bear went up twice as fast as any man could, and quite as well as any monkey that ever I saw."

On natural enemies: "Many hunters have told me that the panther is a desperate and dangerous enemy to the black bear. . . . One hunter heard the long wailing and bawling of a black bear, and, crawling near, expected to see the creature in a trap. But no! He had backed as far as possible into a slight hollow in a hillside, where, furthermore, his rear was protected by a tree, and was vigorously defending himself against the onset of two panthers. The bear was obviously at a great disadvantage, and, without doubt, the panthers would have killed and devoured him; but the hunter interfered by shooting one of the assailants. Before he could reload, the other panther and the bear disappeared in the woods."

Bears of the Northeast Wilderness have little to fear from panthers these days. The human hunter has always been a natural enemy, however, and still is. Also, bears are their own natural enemies. Seton reports his Indian guide ". . . tracked a very big bear in the snow to where it had hunted out another that was already denned up, and had devoured it all but the jaws. The big fellow had feasted for two days, sleeping in the den of the victim and coming out only to eat, or else to drop dung, of which there was an immense quantity outside."

It has been well documented everywhere that boar black bears will eat cub black bears if at all given the opportunity.

Seton on black bear intelligence: "There is little doubt that the bear is high in the scale of mentality, though it cannot compare with a dog, fox, or wolf. It is gifted with marvellous powers of smell and hearing, and has a deep-rooted shyness about all things strange, or doubtful; which saves it again and again from traps of various kinds. Its fixed, safe, and saving motto is: 'In case of doubt, RUN,' and it is nearly always in doubt."

A bear is forever wandering in the spring, the summer, and the fall, searching for food. Although bruin prefers wilderness areas of forest if he can find food there, if he is hungry enough he will establish residence in farm country adjacent to wilderness areas and make opening gambits each day into whatever seems most available and ripe in the cornucopia. As Seton says, "A list of the bear's staples, is not a list of what it likes, but of what it can get." This makes sense to the uneducated bear. It makes more sense than tearing apart an old tree stump and picking out grubs, which is work. Corn is delicious. All you have to do is knock down a few stalks here and a few stalks there and trample back and forth and eat what you like or just sample. Oats have a crunchy, sweet and sour tang. You can wade through them and roll in them, too. Apple trees are made for breaking the branches off of, aren't they? It is remarkable how apples go in and out of your digestive system so fast!

And bears do like honey. Or is it honeybees they like? In any case, often bruin ends up eating both—angry bees swarming about his eyes and mouth, stinging where they can, and bruin bawling with pain, but eating honey, honeybees, wax, grubs . . . everything at once. When hounds chase a bear or hunters fire projectiles or farmers blast away, a bear gets educated—it gets dead or smart. Sometimes a smart bear will accept the dangers of farmcountry living, becoming simply devious in its depredations. Unfortunately sometimes a farmcountry bear will get desperately hungry in the spring and kill and drag off a calf, a sheep, or a goat. Indeed, I imagine a live goat—one that goes baa-baa—would be very attractive in the spring even to a wilderness bear.

CHAPTER 4

If bruin isn't as intelligent as a dog, fox, or wolf,
perhaps he has more "mystical intuition."

A BLACK bear cub weighs 12 ounces at birth. Cubs are born mid-January in Maine and in New Brunswick—from one to four in a litter, but usually two. The cubs weigh from five to eight pounds when they leave the den at three months of age. By the time they go into hibernation in November or December, the cubs weigh 35 to 40 pounds. They den up with their mother and associate with her until the June or July mating season—at which point they must learn to live by themselves. The black bear gestation period is 7 to 7^1/$_2$ months. Most likely a female will mate as early as 3^1/$_2$ but usually 4^1/$_2$ and produce only a single cub. Very likely a male will have to wait until he is a prime 4^1/$_2$ or 5^1/$_2$ before he can secure the affections of a female and fight off males that are older and just as strong. Telemetry data from several sources indicate that a vigorous male services several more than one female during the June and July mating season. A male bear appears slavishly loyal to his receptive females at this time, but by August neither he nor any particular sow could care less about each other. Black bear gestation is unusual in that the fertilized ovum develops only slightly at first and does not attach itself to the uterine wall until almost denning time. But after that it develops rapidly. If a female is in poor condition when she dens, due to injury or malnutrition, the fertilized ovum doesn't develop. A bear is not a true hibernator, everyone says, but certainly is a good sleeper. A sow knows when she has given birth to her cubs and is not unattentive to them. Biologists do take the precaution, before entering dens in the winter, to tranquilize their adult subjects. I have heard that several Maine biologists have actually tasted black bear milk, but I have been unable to get information beyond that rumor.

There are eighteen subspecies of black bear—all in Alaska, Canada, the United States, and as far south as northern Mexico. Good habitat is sea level to 7,000 feet—with mature stands of softwood and hardwood, dense thickets, open areas with berry bushes and grasses, and a plentiful supply of water.

Three-quarters of a bear's diet is vegetation and fruit—mostly leaves and grasses in the spring; berries and wild cherries in the summer; apples, acorns and beechnuts in the fall. A bear will eat carrion enthusiastically in the spring, but with less haste in the summer and fall. It will eat insects—grubs, ants, bees—in the spring, summer and fall. Of course a bear will eat anything appealing, probably including domestic animals, such as sheep or goat, and garbage; but grasses, fruits, insects, and most crops are the major menu items.

As indicated, bear meat is only marginally accepted—even by dogs and cats. This seems to be the case even when bear meat is cooked. I have never made a scientific study of the phenomena involved and I can only cite non-selective experiences. My beagle, Boone, will not eat raw bear meat. He enjoys well-done bear hamburg, however, with lots of garlic. A German shepherd I know will not eat bear meat either raw or well-done with garlic. My five shorthaired cats walk away from a plate of raw bear hamburg. (One cat actually runs away.) My longhaired cat, Troy, ferociously attacks any kind of bear meat raw or cooked. My wife's taxidermied cat doesn't eat anything, of course.

My children think bear meat is delicious—cooked, thank God. My wife cheerfully prepares bear meat, but she is a little picky eating it, I have noticed. We have arguments regarding her attitude.

Of course bear fat rendered into oil is very useful as a shortening. Bear grease is good for waterproofing leather and as a patch lubrication for muzzle-loading rifles. I have known hunters (at least three individuals) to use commercial shortening in warm weather as a patch lubricant only to have it melt into the powder and render their firearms useless. Bear grease has a higher melting point than shortening—and it is what Daniel Boone used when he didn't use spit.

There are an estimated 250,000 black bear in the United States. Canada has perhaps twice that many. Alaska and Washington have the largest U.S. populations. In the northeastern U.S., Maine has the highest population. Quebec and New Brunswick must have very high bear numbers, but biologists there have never counted bears carefully because they don't consider bruin very important. They do know, however, that a bear population interacts with a moose population: i.e., that mature bear love to eat upon calf moose.

Manly Hardy believed that bears kill adult moose and interact with the deer herd, too. He had this to say in 1901:

"As you wish me to state some instances of bears killing moose, and also of their carrying away deer before eating them, I will give you two instances.

"In the fall of 1859, I carried William H. Staples to Chesuncook in my canoe, as I was on my way to Caucomgomock for a fall hunt. Mr. Staples joined his partner, Allen B. Farrar, at Chamberlain. On coming out of the woods after the hunt was over I saw them both and both told me, that in November when there was several inches of snow, Mr. Staples found where a bear had crept up to a large bull moose which was lying down, had jumped upon his neck and held him down till he had killed the moose by biting his neck. The bull had as he expressed it, flounced around over quite a space on his side, but never regained his feet. The bear made a small track and was evidently not over two years old, while the moose had nine prongs on each horn.

"Jonathan Darling told me then, when going up a branch of the Aroostook, on coming round a bend, he came upon a she bear and two cubs feeding on a cow moose just killed. He said that the bank was quite high and the bear had evidently jumped from the bank upon the moose which was feeding in the water.

"I have known several cases where bears have come to persons calling moose, evidently expecting to catch the moose. If any more proof is needed I will say that among the hundreds of moose hides I have had tanned by the Indians, I have seen quite a number which showed plainly where a bear had seized them on each side of the hips, and every claw mark showed for from a foot to 18 inches in length. In most cases when the first grip failed to hold, they had been seized a second or third time, and where the claw marks came together on the lower part of the thigh the scars were one or two inches wide. We have no animal except a bear which could do this, and these moose were seized when standing and the long gashes showed they were trying to escape. No one who knows anything of the quickness of a bear will question that where some escaped, many were seized who were not so fortunate.

"In regard to their carrying off deer to quiet places before eating them: I once about the first of June, found where a bear had taken a very large buck which was lying near an old logging road. I followed a long ways where he had dragged his deer. In several places where the deer had caught on firs as large as one's wrist they had been torn out by the roots. I found the deer lying on the edge of a gully. I went to the house of a farmer who hunted some and told him where to find the deer, and he set for the bear and caught him.

"Mr. D.P. Wood, formerly of Baskehegan, (Drew Plantation I think it was called) told me that he shot a large deer near the edge of an old field—while he was gone for a team to haul the deer home—a bear carried the deer off by walking on his hind feet so that although he searched a long time he could not find a trace of it."

The average Northeast Wilderness black bear in good habitat has an autumn weight of 100 to 300 pounds. Males are larger than females. The average length is between four and six feet. The average height is about three feet.

Roundworm and trichinae are the most common parasitic afflictions. Actually every single freshly killed black bear I have seen had roundworms crawling out of its body cavity. On the other hand, I have seen none, that when examined closely, showed any evidence (laboratory tested) of trichinae.

Manly Hardy believed, contrary to Seton, that bears were smarter than wolves. In 1908 he wrote:

". . . [Bears] . . . not only reason, but are progressive. Fifty years ago a great many bears in Maine were taken in log traps. Gradually it became more and more rare that one would enter a log trap, yet there was no trouble in taking them in steel traps set in houses of logs or brush, but they soon learned to avoid going in by the front entrance and would tear out the side of the house and get the bait, leaving the trap set. Some bears, like some people, could easily be fooled once, but unlike many people, it was seldom one was fooled a second time. A man will go into a gambling house and lose his money and keep on going and not ever learn to avoid one; but a bear, after he has been once trapped, is very seldom caught in a trap set in the same way.

"I know of a case where, after trying all known ways to trap a bear, a place was found where there was a cavity in a ledge shaped like an inverted V. A large bait was placed at the further end and a trap at the entrance, the clog being shoved inside and perfectly covered; and, as the entrance was too wide for the trap to fill it, a piece of an old beech log was stood at one side, between the trap and the end of the clog. Everything looked perfectly natural and showed no signs. The trap could not be taken out without throwing the beech log down unless that was first removed. Instead of entering as was expected, the bear removed the beech log first, throwing it to one side; then, taking hold of the end of the clog, he drew out that and the trap and hauled them to a safe distance, leaving the trap still set, and then went in and secured the bait. It is not known that this bear was ever caught in a trap.

"In four cases I have known bears caught in steel traps to climb trees, and, after entangling the clog in the long branches, to throw themselves down, trusting to their weight to pull them out of the trap. In one case this worked successfully; in another the bear escaped with the loss of a toe; in the other two cases the bears were found dead. In one case which I saw, the ground under the tree, a large hemlock, looked as if the tree had been struck by lightning from the amount of bark and limbs the bear had torn off.

"I once set a trap for a large bear. Having heard that others had failed I took particular precautions. I selected a place where three large pines stood in almost an equilateral triangle. I set the trap between the trees which were nearest together, leaving the other for the back of the house, and endwise between this tree and those on the sides, placed short pieces of old logs, which the loggers had used to skid between rocks. As bears dislike to touch anything prickly I banked the wall on both sides and covered the top with large old dry spruce boughs until it looked like a brush heap, and all around outside stuck small spruce trees, cut a long distance from the spot. Except for the bait I think few men would have suspected that anything had been placed there by a man.

"The first time the trap was looked at a porcupine had been caught by the tail, and the bear had dragged him and the trap out and had torn him out. The second time the spruce boughs were found taken down from one side, and the logs tossed aside, the bait taken, and the trap left undisturbed. One log, a piece of watersoaked juniper, which was a good load for a man to lift, had been struck with one paw and sent several yards away. The trap was looked at until too late in the spring to catch bears, but the bear did not come again. Being ashamed to be beaten by a bear, the next fall—although in going and coming I had to travel over thirty miles to look at the trap—I set it again. I set two traps without bait. One was on a level intervale between a large spruce and a birch whose roots were raised above the ground and reached across to the spruce, making a place for the bear to step over. I set it as carefully as for an otter, scented with beaver oil and rubbed scorched honey on the trees high up.

"At the second look, the clog was found on the opposite side of the birch from where it had been placed, tucked under the birch roots. There were marks of a struggle and the trap, twisted all out of shape, lay near it. But what was singular, a deep trail where the clog had been dragged led away from the trap. It was evident that the bear had been caught by the hind foot. He had started off with the trap, and in the course of a quarter of a mile had found two large cedars turned up by the wind, but still green. Beginning at the top of each of them he had limbed both trees from top to bottom, breaking off green limbs as large as a man's wrist. Then, not finding any chance to get fast to anything, he evidently remembered the place where he was caught, and, circling back, had shoved the end of the clog under the roots of the birch, and, exerting his great strength, had wrecked the trap in a way a horse would not have had the strength to do. It took a blacksmith to put that trap in shape again."

For most people any contact with a bear comes as a shock or as a surprise. It is either a pleasant shock or an unpleasant surprise. Even people hunting black bear have a sense of shock at a sighting—because the black bear always has dignity and power regardless of its actions. It could be scratching itself—in the businesslike manner of a large dog; or sitting on its backside and swinging its head—looking like a fat man listening to Mozart; or it could be defacating—which it does ungracefully.

For thrills you can't beat having a bear brushing against your tent in the night. Of course, this has happened to me.

"What is going on?" my companion asked.

"There's a bear outside!" I was out of my sleeping bag and trying to string my recurve bow. "He just brushed against the tent! Didn't you hear him?"

"You got your foot on my face."

I finally managed to string my bow and nock a good arrow with a sharp broadhead.

I peered out the back window of the tent, which only permitted a 90-degree view of the gravel pit where we were situated, but included a vision of several sacks of bait for bear hunting piled 20 feet away. I could smell the bait—fresh beef and pork bones and fat—mingled with the ever-green odors of the Maine northcountry in the springtime. The moon was bright and each limb of every tree was silhouetted sharply against the illuminated snow in the forest beyond the gravel pit.

Then my hair stood on end. Hair really does stand on end in certain kinds of threatening situations. My side of the tent had slowly bulged inward. I had heard quick exhalations and heavy grinding of pebbles. The tent jerked. A guy rope strummed. Then I saw the bear.

"He's stealing a bag of bait."

"I guess he is."

"Well, what's one bag of bait, more or less."

"Right."

We were peering out the back window of the tent, watching the bear shuffle off, the sack of bait swinging from his jaws. When his right side moved the bag swung left, and when he moved his left side, the bag swung right. He moved into the forest beyond the gravel pit, becoming a huge silhouette among the trees against the illuminated snow. He dropped the bag and commenced feeding in plain view of us.

"He's either crazy," I said, "or mystical intuition is telling him he's perfectly safe from any harm we could do him."

"Well, he's not crazy," my companion said.

CHAPTER 5

*Scouting and hunting for bear without the services of a bear guide
is usually not productive.*

YOU almost have to consult a lawyer to hunt bears legally in
any of the states or provinces of the Northeast Wilderness.
For example, in New Brunswick there is a spring season. In
Maine there is not. You can't bait bear in Vermont. You
can't trap bear or hunt bear with dogs in New Brunswick.
Professional bear guiding is no longer allowed in New
Hampshire. In Canada, a nonresident must hunt with a
guide. There are different kinds of guides in Canada. Some
can take out only one person and can't be paid for their
services. Others may take out two or three—depending on
the province—and they must be paid a minimum wage, and
they possibly expect more money under the table either
before, during, or after the hunt. In New York the law
doesn't say that you can bait bear, but it doesn't say that you
can't. And bear hunting laws keep changing from year to
year. By the time you are reading this the states and provinces
could have swapped around their bear regulations from what
they are now, as I am writing, and even added new ones: i.e.,
a spring season in Maine but none in New Brunswick, etc.;
or the whiskey bottle in outhouse must be presumed to be
personal property of guide and no one else, etc.

If you are going to hunt bear on your own, know the rules and regulations of the sport in the state or province of your recreation. Always go by the current law book. Last year's law book is never quite the same.

If you feel slightly paranoid because you are a gun owner and a hunter, have your gun in a locked case when you travel. If you're travelling to Canada, leave your hand-gun at home. Handguns are illegal there. If you're travelling to Maine, have your .44 Super Blackhawk in a locked case, same as you would a shotgun or a rifle. Then that guy in the car with the whirling blue roof lights in Massachusetts won't be hard on you—if you happen to be going slightly over 65 or something like that. Chances are he's a hunter, also—and chances are he owns more guns than that one revolver hanging from his hip.

If you intend to hunt bear over bait, I advise you to hire a guide. A guide will know where to place baits to attract bears—not irate landowners.

If you intend to hunt bear with your dogs, hire a public relations expert. Or better, leave your dogs home, and hire a guide with his dogs.

If you intend to hunt bear by still-hunting in old apple orchards or on beechnut ridges, I wish you all the luck in the world. When the leaves on the ground are like cornflakes and you have to make noises simulating squirrels and birds or when the fog is thick and you can hardly see and from every twig there hangs a drop of water—certainly the situation is challenging and demanding of stealth, skill, and strength. These are the traditional aptitudes of hunting.

If you want to scout for bear and hunt them down on your own, then boreal New England and New York are the only places legally open for you in the Northeast Wilderness. Maine is a bargain and convenient for hunters coming from the north or the south. Maine has Interstate 95—which presently will cost a car-load of hunters about a $3 toll from below Portland up to Augusta. Then from beyond Augusta about 200 more miles up to Houlton, this scenic ribbon is free. And, of course, for Canadians from the north, I-95 is even less expensive. Besides, I-95 is like a zoo. Moose trot along the edges. Deer browse just beyond the guardrails. Also, it is alleged, coyotes have special places of convenience on I-95 where they sit panting, waiting for roadkills.

Maine is less of a bargain, but certainly handier, if a hunter buys a ride on an airplane into Bangor. Of course many sportsmen find the toil of driving three or four days from Alabama, for example, hardly worth any hunting trip. My cousin, who lives in West Virginia, each year drives to Colorado with a buddy for an elk hunt. Each year he swears is his last, because they arrive bug-eyed and white-knuckled and they return that way, albeit usually with an elk. But they could fly and save time—but not money—and the elk could fly, too. Same with sportsmen coming to Maine. They could fly and save time, and the bear could fly, also. Delta Airlines goes into Bangor International Airport several times a day. Bar Harbor Airlines does likewise. And a car may be rented at the terminal building.

Professional guides and outfitters are the best sources for information on where exactly to hunt black bear.

I once asked Maine guide and real-estate entrepreneur, Ron Masure of Greenville, where he would advise the independent bear hunter to go scouting for bear in Maine. "This place takes in a lot of acres," Masure said. "If you drew a 50 mile radius around Greenville, even more, you would have some of the best bear habitat that has received the least pressure. Of course Patten and Jackman are well known. Indeed they are fine. North of Greenville and Rockwood—some five or six million acres—and west of Baxter State Park there's lots of country that never ever has seen a bear hunter."

And it's big country, too. The kind of country you really don't want to get lost in, but if you want to go sneaking over beechnut ridges and hunting bear that way, you must expect to become confused. Actually that's no big deal and you shouldn't be ashamed of yourself or embarrassed. A lot of good woodsmen have been lost, or at least stuck overnight in the woods. I have, for example.

My situation was trivial. The kind of common circumstance the average hunter dreads most: bewildered in the bush at dark, not exactly lost, but certainly not sure at all where he is. Being really, truly seriously lost has a certain dignity to it—add a dash of hypothermia or a mad moose or a bad bear and you have a story to tell your grandchildren or sell to the Reader's Digest. But being immobilized in the wild blackness overnight is just plain embarrassing.

No road traffic noise and no chainsaws sputtering did I hear. The sky was thickly clouded and to detect the direction of sunset was impossible. So I didn't know where west was. When night came I didn't know where north was either—because of the gloomy cloak hiding the stars.

I decided I would be logical—i.e., I'd stay put, rig a bed, protect my dead deer from coyotes and build a fire. Unfortunately I didn't have the means to kindle any flame.

It was opening day of the Maine archery season. I had overslept in the morning and dashed out the door insufficiently outfitted—no compass, knife, matches, etc. Just my bow and my quiver full of arrows. I had shot a deer, broken my glasses and injured my knee, and I didn't find my fat trophy until late in the afternoon.

I was lost in central Maine. (Central and southern Maine is farms and woodlands—you take a short hike from a house and you are deer hunting.) Much of northern Maine is big woods—very remote commercial forest land with hundreds of miles of logging roads and many navigable rivers and streams—containing no facilities. A hunter needs a 4X4, a canoe, and a tent. A large portion of the north is also vast commercial forest land mixed with agricultural land and woodlands. If a hunter had a pickup camper that would be adequate. Fewer hunters get lost in the big woods than in farm country in Maine. People get lost when they don't carry the basics in their pockets because they are close to home—the basics being a handy item that tells you where north is, a marvelous tool that can cut and slice, and some magic that can make a fire.

But I knew a lost person could do nothing right and still survive just because he desired life. A lost person so dehydrated that his lacerations do not bleed could struggle on mindless and naked until he was saved. That's what I told myself. In any case, I could abandon the deer, and with my flashlight hobble in a straight line in any direction and come to a road—and be saved. I would avoid embarrassment, save my wife from worry, and not have to confront my imagination concerning coyotes.

The night would not be particularly cold, I thought. Perhaps into the low forties. A fire would provide a beacon. (A fire is a cheerful friend when you are lost and provides warmth.) In my bag of photo gear (not with me at that time) I have a waxed bundle of matches, flint and steel and charred cloth, and a pad of steel wool. Usually when I'm with other hunters, I make sure everyone carries with him into the woods a pad of steel wool and a flashlight. Everyone appreciates the flashlight and former Boy Scouts know that if you hold two flashlight batteries, top touching bottom with some shredded-out steel wool under the bottom battery and touching the top battery, the steel wool will burn.

I had no scouring pad, however. I thought that I could perhaps get sparks by striking a broadhead against a rock. Attempts with various hard rocks failed. The broadheads I had with me were the replaceable stainless type. I knew that the old style Bear Razorhead would spark on rocks and with one of them I could have ignited tinder into flame. In Maine or anywhere in the Northeast Wilderness the best kindling is birch bark curls and twigs from evergreens.

But I was in the woods insufficiently outfitted. The sun was down. My glasses were broken. My knee hurt. I wished it were possible somehow, maybe, perchance, God willing, to start a fire.

At 5:56 the woods began to blacken. To pass the time I had gathered kindling: dead fir and spruce tips and twigs and birch bark. I looked around for bird nests, but couldn't find any. I collected plenty of dry wood. I was hoping for a bolt of lightning—a brilliant thought or some static electricity from heaven so that I could create a fire. Here I was—an expert woodsman stranded among trees for a night and I couldn't make a fire. My wife must be starting to worry, I thought. Probably close to midnight I would hear a small airplane buzzing.

At 6:02 I tried the flashlight. It worked very well. I gathered a huge pile of dry leaves.

No fire, but at least I could stay put and build a shelter beneath a nearby blowdown. I cleaned out under the blowdown and covered one side thickly with boughs torn from pines. The affair when finished resembled a bear's den—and I had seen quite a few of those. At least I'm as smart as a bear, I thought. Then I moved the leaves inside and hauled my dead deer closer and off the ground on top of my firewood. I was extremely thirsty, but I would have to forget about that. I was also hungry. For supper my wife had planned to cook a fat rooster and for us to drink a bottle of cold chablis.

I crawled into my den.

Soon I began thinking about coyotes. Coyotes kill large animals—they attack head on with canines cutting for lost woodsmen's jugulars. Deer make up at least 10% of what coyotes eat. Apples make up another percentage. I had seen coyotes clean up the drops under a Cortland once. Surely they must prefer meat to fruit. I didn't doubt that a freshly dead deer must be an invitation to coyotes for supper.

I crawled out of my den and applied scent camouflage lotion to the deer and to my clothing. Whether this was logical or useless I don't know. But fears are always eased by actions—and possibly what I did was a manifestation of hysteria. Man is an animal and can live in a den and survive weeks without food. However, in an anxiety situation, his fears are what he thinks about.

Act logically when afraid, I ordered myself.

I turned on the flashlight. No yellow eyes looking at me. A skunk has red eyes when you shine a light. I imagined a coyote has yellow. The time was 7:56. I crawled into my leaves inside my den again and forced myself to dream—in the beginning—of chicken and chablis. I can't recall my other dreams.

"I don't understand why the airplane didn't see the fire," my wife said the next day at supper—which was biscuits with two chickens and two bottles of wine.

"I told you a fire was impossible," I said.

"And you were not where you said you would be," she said.

"And I was in the woods unprepared."

"Oh, the scoutmaster called this afternoon. He wants you to give a talk to the boys about how to get lost."

"What about?"

"About how to get lost."

"I'm sure I could say something," I said.

CHAPTER 6

Searching for a bear guide you might discover a hero.

HUNTING bruin with dogs or hunting bruin over established baits is more productive by far than still-hunting bruin. Hunters can enjoy any of the three methods, however. Bear guides offer their dogs or established baits to hunters for a fee, but seldom seem willing to take clients walking and stalking over beechnut ridges in the fall or along streams where suckers run in the spring. Guides feel that clients are too seldom satisfied or successful hunting bears in ambulatory situations, as they would be hunting other game animals. As Seton indicated, guides know the problem with bears is bruin's "deep-rooted shyness about all things strange or doubtful." Anyway, there's no money in it for guides when hunters go off on their own; and no significant money in it, either, when a guide takes one client still-hunting.

If you really want a bear you should search for a bear guide. The most certain, methodical way to find a good bear guide is to read the ads in several hunting magazines, and make a list of the bear guides in business in the state or province where you would most like to hunt. Knowing in general where you want to hunt is like solving half the problem. For example, as I'm writing this I am feeling a strong impulse to bowhunt moose in Quebec. Probably a major factor in my wanting to experience Quebec is simply to practice my high-school French. "Parlez-vous anglais?" I will ask de guide. After he shrug his shouldeurs, I will ask, "Veuillez me montrer le grand moose sur cette carte." De guide, he grin. "Je vous demande pardon," de guide, he say, pointing at de two ear of him, indicating that he doesn't understand what I am demanding. I can hardly wait to bow-hunt moose in Quebec.

After you have made your list of bear guides in the area you want to hunt, the best thing to do is to write them all letters asking for information. The truly professional guides will respond to your letters within two weeks. The others are perhaps professional, but they are disorganized or they don't need your business. After you've received several brochures or whatever, then you get on the telephone and call up the guides who sent you the most interesting information.

Assuming you're to hunt over bait, you ask each guide the following questions: How many hunters do you take during a season? How many active baits do you maintain during a season? Do your hunters hunt with rifles, pistols, or bows? What percentage of each? What is your guide-to-hunter ratio? How many of your active baits produce more than one bear a season? What kind of bait do you use—fish scraps, meat scraps, sweets? How often do you bait? In your last season, what percentage of your hunters saw mature bears while hunting during legal hunting hours?

If you're to hunt with dogs, find out the breed of the guide's pack. The Plott has been selectively bred for North-east Wilderness bear hunting. In any case, check out Lady, Spike, Mopsy, and Thor and how they perform in chasing situations. This is best done by talking with a few of the guide's former clients—his references. The guide's pack doesn't have to be Plott to be good. Hunting bruin with hounds is exciting and may involve exercise. With respect to this the guide should check out the hunter to make sure he is capable of vigorous exertion. The usual procedure with dogs is for everyone to run stumbling through the woods to the tree where the bear rests near the tiptop, then to withdraw the hounds to relative safety and then—if you are the designated hunter—you have to be ready to shoot. The bear may escape in the interim, but don't worry because the hounds probably will tree him again soon and you'll have another chance, after additional aerobic sprinting through the forest. Also, because most guides are conservationists rather than game-hogs, the opinion may be offered that a particular bear is not an appropriate trophy. In those instances the best thing to do is allow the bear to escape and look for another. A reputable guide should assure his clients there are plenty of good bears in the woods.

The image of a professional guide that most people have is of a hard working fellow during bird, bear and deer hunting seasons, and early salmon season just after ice-out, and perhaps for a week or so early in June when the bass are nesting. When not hired out to assist non-residents in the productive pursuit of game and fish, the image of an "idle" professional guide is of an itinerant carpenter, plumber, electrician, nature artist, trapper, outdoor writer, and perhaps someone who sits at a sock-making machine knitting thick woolies his wife sells at craft fairs along with her own hand-knit angora mittens. Believe me, this latter image isn't far off the mark. The professional guide is too principled and conservative to make ends meet in a manner that would compromise his independence. And show me a professional guide who uses food stamps and I'll show you a terribly embarrassed individual.

By tradition, the business of guiding in Maine has never been big business. If you visit from out of Maine, or if you come from Portland, and you need help hunting, fishing, canoeing, wilderness camping, even bicycle touring, you hire a guide much as you hire a lawyer to write a will or compose a binding contract—much as you visit a doctor to lance a boil or correct a problem you might have with hemorrhoids.

The lawyer prevents the bank from foreclosing on your mortgage. The doctor prescribes a change of diet to help correct your hemorrhoids. These guys are heroes. By tradition lawyers and doctors are not big business men. The professional guide is a demigod to his sport who landed a forty pound salmon. And he is a paladin to his hunter who bowbagged a giant 500 pound black bear. However, his special role is to provide situations in which weary people can appreciate themselves as biological organisms in a natural world—on the lakes, in the woods, or in circumstances elsewhere that soothe with vigor the fear we have of death and dying. Wayne Bosowicz is that kind of professional guide.

We had been planning a rabbit hunt together for quite some time. Before Christmas there hadn't been enough snow. After Christmas it was too cold—too cold for Wayne to travel down to my place and too cold for me to drive up to Dover-Foxcroft in a rusty, old Jap pickup with bald tires. Besides, my beagle has a habit of getting lost in new territory. But coyotes are consuming most of the rabbits in my hunting areas, so I had no choice but to head up north.

Wayne said he was sure he could find a spot his coyotes didn't know about yet. We were to hunt with archery gear, and we figured we needed an area fairly thick with bunnies.

It was Wednesday—bitter cold and the wind whistled through the hole in my windshield and I had to put my coat over Boone because he was shivering violently. Wednesday was Wayne's fast day. For health reasons one day each week he consumes nothing but water. "Let me show you my new broadhead, Norm," Wayne said when I was finally inside his warm kitchen sipping coffee. He was obviously anxious to attack the snowshoe hares, but the man has compassion: first it was okay if I thawed out my frozen body.

The "new broadhead" was a dummy hand-grenade drilled to fit the end of a 2219 aluminum arrow. A good joke. "Ha!" Wayne exclaimed, appreciating my mild amusement. He retired the arrow to a closet and then filled a glass with water at the kitchen sink.

"Aren't you hungry?" I asked.

"I could almost eat a bear, Norm . . . ha!"

The Maine guide is a celebrated romantic figure in the folklore of American history. Old time Maine guides were measured by how far they could walk in the woods without getting lost and by how hard they could paddle a loaded canoe without swamping. Modern Maine guides are measured by their ability to manage four-wheel-drive vehicles without getting stuck, and motorboats, rafts, seaplanes— and by their ability to market their goods and services in a cost-effective, business-like manner. They must use modern business methods—bank financing, computer management . . . the whole bit.

"I have a carpenter here now," Wayne said, "adding to my home so I can have an office for my new electronic typewriter and wastepaper shredder, ha! If a business doesn't grow, it dies. Honestly, that's a fact of life these days. The old guides had it made, believe me. They had fewer headaches, ha!"

Fishing guides use sophisticated electronics to locate the best spot for a client to wet a line. Hunting guides (bear hunting guides) use dogs with telemetric collars which emit beeper signals. Bear guides get nervous when they can't get a fix on their valuable hounds. The special collars may inform the handlers where the dogs may have a bear up a tree, but more important they inform where the dogs are. This distinction is significant.

Bosowicz's fame is as a bear hunter. It all began for him more than twenty years ago when he started breeding Plott hounds. He entered his hounds in coon hunting competitions in West Virginia, Mississippi, New York, and in other states—but he was spending more money than he was making. "My family had no peas in their pea soup," he says. Fortunately Plott hounds take naturally to running bear, so in 1976 Bosowicz plunged into the bear guiding business full-time.

The phone rang several times while I sat sipping coffee and getting warm. Hunters were calling in from all over the country making bookings for spring bear hunts in Ontario and asking questions about fall hunts in Maine. "It's hard to sell Maine," Wayne says. "I have to stand on my head and do tricks like a trained seal, dump money into ads in magazines. It's unbelievable. We've had political business with bears for years in this state and the hunters have a funny taste in their mouths as a result. I remember when I had Germans booked and the season was cancelled. No one can get a German over here now for love or money, ha!"

He poured me another cup of coffee and helped himself to more water. The phone calls were winding him up, so to speak. Bear, bear, bear . . . a topic hard to dislodge from foremost in his thoughts and conversation. "Ontario is great. I get letters and phone calls all the time about Ontario. Can they hunt there in the spring? Can they hunt there in the fall?"

He began walking back and forth from where I sat to the phone, as if expecting it to ring as he talked. I was beginning to wonder how on earth, at that moment, I could dislodge him from bear, bear, bear so we could go rabbit hunting.

"Don't you have an answering machine?" I asked.

"No," he said, his eyes twinkling. "They hang up on a machine. I tried that."

My glasses were no longer fogged up. I put them on and regarded Bosowicz carefully: gray beard, barrel chest, broomstick legs, and fifty years old. He'll make a fine looking Santa Claus when he's sixty, I decided. But he'll have bears instead of reindeer pulling his sleigh.

I had no doubt that this award-winning Maine guide deserved unusual recognition: knowledgeable concerning the game animal his clients pursued and conscientious in his business and treatment of his clients; always willing to go the extra mile, show the extra care, give the extra service. Precision Shooting Equipment has dubbed him, "the standard bearer for every outfitter to admire." Every year that company picks a guide they most admire—and they picked Wayne in 1979 and 1980. Two years in a row. An unusual occurance, to say the least. PSE may be self-serving in its motives for picking an outfitter like that every year. That's the American way of conducting business, however—and

PSE makes awful fine archery equipment and Wayne Bo-sowicz is, in fact, "the standard bearer." "God, guns, and guts built this country," Wayne says, "and let's keep it that way."

In Maine—and in Ontario—Wayne utilizes a large territory for bear hunting. This is probably the reason why he offers quality bear hunting—or "bears hanging from the game pole," as he says. The extra care and service would be meaningless if it were not for a good bear population in a large territory. Wayne's hunting area spreads out at least 70 miles in all directions from his headquarters near Dover-Foxcroft. And always, when the law is on the bears, he is foraging looking for new areas. "New" areas, by the way, are always territories unclaimed by other bear guides. "A client likes to feel he's in the wilderness—just him and some bears. No other bear guide with other hunters. When one bear guide goes into another's territory, it's bad business for both of them. A client tells his friends back home and the next year you're dead in Syracuse, New York . . . ha!"

He spoke in a tone that was soft and apologetic. "Maine is one of the most wild and remote regions left in our country. Maine has 20 million acres of forest covering 90% of the state. Where I work in Maine, we produce the largest bear in the state. In Ontario the bear population must be close to the highest in the world. I have walk-in freezers both places. I don't guarantee a kill and I don't guarantee the weather, but I do guarantee a good time. In Ontario, even though the season opens in April, we do not start until prime time as I'm extremely serious about production. The 1986 price of our bait hunts was $785. Hound hunts were $950 per person for two hunters or more."

"That was reasonable," I agreed.

"Very reasonable . . . . I got four guides working, bait to buy, gas, insurance, vehicles to pay for and things, advertising . . . ha! . . . other things to pay for you wouldn't believe . . . but the bear have been good to me."

"You've been good to the bear," I said. "Because you hunt them so well, the bear is respected and appreciated as a game animal. He didn't use to be."

"Ha! . . . I put the bear into politics. That's a good one. Fantastic! I'm more interested in having game around for tomorrow than in making a buck today. That's true! The last thing I'd like to see is no game, no bear around for my son to hunt, or for your son. There's 1000 guides in Maine now. Six hundred make money out of it. Three hundred make most of their income out of it. There's not one hunting guide who wouldn't give up his money for the game."

"Was it easy when you got your license?"

"Are you kidding? It used to be easy to get a license. Now a guide has to be physically fit, know CPR, first-aid, what a brown trout looks like, how to get lost, ha! . . . He might as well go to college!"

"Let's go rabbit hunting," I said.

"I'm hungry," Wayne said.

"Think of your health," I said.

A bell seemed to ring in his head. He brightened and smiling he slapped his pockets looking for something. Eventually he produced a small plastic bottle and tossed it to me. "Let's use this scent on rabbits. It works great on deer and bear."

I squirted some from the bottle onto a paper towel, then applied the dampened towel to my woolen pants over my knees. Wayne did the same. We collected our bows and the dog and headed out.

At first we noted more coyote sign than anything else. Eventually, however, we came to an area of low-growing hemlock and fir—and rabbit droppings and trails in the snow everywhere. I released the dog.

In about ten seconds Boone had a rabbit going. He yowled excitedly; the rabbit raced, cut left and disappeared. The first circle the rabbit made I shot and missed. The second circle—as the rabbit paused ten yards from him— Wayne released an accurate arrow.

As a Maine guide, Bosowicz is a living, breathing champion. The first famous Maine guide was the Penobscot Indian Thoreau hired in 1846 to show him the way from Bangor to the Allagash Lakes and back. His name was Joe Polis, and he charged Thoreau a dollar and a half a day, plus fifty cents a week for his canoe. And he demanded certain hunting opportunities: "Me want to get some moose," this early hero had said.

CHAPTER 7

The equipment needed for a black bear hunt can be anything
from a 4X4 to a chocolate bar. But first consideration must be
given to the problem of human scent, scents black bears associate
with hunter-presence, masking scents, and attracting scents.

I AGREE with Seton's observation that the black bear is
"gifted with marvellous powers of smell." But simply
knowing that bruin has the best nose of any critter in the
woods is not going to do you much good unless you take
action to acknowledge that fact. Certainly if you are going
to still-hunt bear or hunt bear over bait you're going to have
a problem with scent. However, if you are going to hunt
with dogs, then scent—your human odor—should not be a
significant concern. Suggest to the guide that he should
really use Old Spice under his arms and he might indicate
that your favorite English pipe tobacco—a choice blend of
Turkish and Cuban leaf—is causing Rex, Sally, Spike, and
Sparkle to regurgitate. Other than that, hunting with dogs
shouldn't present a scent problem.

ITEM: *Hot water for bathing*

Take a shower every day. Motels and most camps have
plenty of hot water. However, at my bear camp in Grand

Lake Stream, Maine, where the guides stay, we must use solar-showers. These are four-ply bags filled with water that we hang up in convenient trees after breakfast when the weather is clear: a clear panel collects the sunlight; a black panel absorbs the sun's energy; a micro cell layer insulates and traps heat; and a silver reflective panel boosts efficiency. The bags have built-in shower heads and on-off controls. I bought them in 1985 at L.L. Bean in Freeport, Maine, for $13.50 each. If the weather is clear, the bags can produce hot water for showers in three hours. If the weather is not clear, we heat up water inside the camp and fill up the bags with that.

ITEM: *Unscented soaps*

Wash yourself with a soap that does not contain a perfume. The best such product that I've come upon is Tink's Non-Scent Camo Soap. This is available from Safariland Hunting Corporation of McLean, Virginia. I don't know how much it costs because Tink Nathan gave me a case of the product long ago and I haven't run out yet—in fact the supply I have on hand now will last my lifetime. The soap comes in large plastic unbreakable bottles and the components are baking soda, chlorophyll, and "a secret ingredient that destroys odor at the molecular level."

You should also wash your dirty bear-hunting clothes with this or a similar camo soap. Commercial laundry detergent found in grocery stores contains cleaning agents, softeners, whiteners, colorants, and perfume. Keep your bear-hunting clothes away from all of them. What you don't want to wash, you should at least air outside in the sun, or store in a bag with pine and cedar branches, and you should certainly not wear your bear hunting clothes when the camp cook is preparing onions, garlic, fish, bacon, asparagus, broccoli, or brussels sprouts. You should also avoid smokers and not smoke yourself when you are bear hunting. When you need gas for your truck, have the station-attendant pump it for you. Many hunters are in the habit of sipping a beer when they're riding around. That's too bad. Usually they spill some on their hunting clothes. If you are not hunting with dogs, avoid dogs. That doggy odor is almost the same danger-signal to bruin's nose as your odor.

ITEM: *Consider chlorophyll tablets*

There is also Tink's Non-Scent Camouflage Tablets. These are for pill-poppers, of course, and I can't bring myself to experiment with a product that might affect my health. However, Tink insists they are absolutely harmless: 16 mg of sodium potassium copper chlorophyllins, 100% water-soluble, in a base of powdered sugar and spearmint oil. According to a great deal of testimony, Tink's formula really works. What it does is deodorize your perspiration. The 100 tablet bottle lasts for two weeks, if you follow directions, which means it's good for a one-week bear-hunt, because you should start taking the pills seven days in advance. Tink says only three days in advance are necessary.

ITEM: *A supply of coyote urine as a masking scent*

Undoubtedly skunk scent is a better masking agent. However, I have never noted the presence of actual skunks in wilderness bear habitat, and as Seton indicated, the black bear possesses a deeply instinctive shyness and perceives the world conservatively. But if you are hunting in farmcountry, skunk scent might be fine. The kind I like the best is the two-solution type (Tex Isbell's Skunk Coverscent) that doesn't stink until you mix it: i.e., twenty drops of each solution on an absorbent material placed downwind of your blind if you're hunting over bait or pinned to your cap if you're still-hunting. This type of skunk scent has been described to me as somewhat of an attracting concoction, too, for use in agricultural habitat, I imagine. This application is worth a try: you dig a shallow hole on the trail the bear travels to your bait and line the bottom with aluminum foil; mix the two solutions on the foil; and cover the hole with just enough sticks and leaves to hide the foil but still allow the skunk scent out. The theory is that when the bear is on his path coming to the bait, he pauses sniffing at the hole long enough for you to shoot him. The hunter should take care where he places the hole, of course, so as to afford himself a good shot.

I have observed numerous coyotes in wilderness areas of Maine and New Brunswick. Coyote urine is a good cover scent for bear hunting, especially if you're hunting over bait. Coyotes frequently visit bear baits just to see what's being offered, but you will seldom see them because they are out circulating mostly at night. They will leave their scent, however, and although bears probably loathe coyotes—they smell almost like a dog, but not quite—bears don't fear coyotes. The best way to use coyote urine is with scent pads that fasten to the soles of your boots. (Safariland Hunting Corporation sells the best kind of scent pads I know of. However, they do not sell coyote urine. You'll have to buy that in a trapping supply store.) With an eyedropper, you saturate the sponges inside the scent pads, and place the pads carefully inside a ziplock plastic bag. When you are about 100 yards from your blind, you take the pads out of the bag and slip them onto your boots, walk to your blind, then put the pads back into the plastic bag again. Don't get the coyote urine on your hands or clothing, especially if you're to climb a tree to your blind. Coyotes don't climb trees and bruin would be suspicious if he smelled coyote urine twenty feet off the ground.

A cover scent that Wayne Bosowicz is particularly enthusiastic about is Pro-Cover, something—naturally—that he himself invented. Being, as he is, a friendly person in the outfitting business, for many years he's spoken to me of a "secret" scent—but never given me any or revealed to me the nature of his concoction until two or three years ago. It smells kind of like sarsparilla and sassafras—and is, you can imagine, far more pleasant to handle than coyote urine. "Putting meat on the meat pole is what pays my bills—nothing else," says Bosowicz—saying it so often that it must be his slogan. "But in the past few years if twenty men came to hunt with me they would all have twenty different bottles of scents and lures and junk. In fact, most of what they had was junk, which was affecting their hunting negatively. So I decided to do something. I developed a mix containing natural ingredients that did the job, that wasn't offensive, so if a bottle accidentally opened in a hunter's suitcase his wife would still do his laundry. It not only hid the hunter, but seemed to attract the game."

Pro-Cover is available at selected sporting goods stores in the United States, but not in Canada. Last I heard, the cost is $4.95 per bottle, but a little goes a long way. Since it seems to attract game, including bear, I prefer using it on a scent rag within shooting distance of a hunter's blind—in the same manner as I would use oil of anise, liquid smoke, etc. The directions on the bottle apply to deer hunters mostly: squirt some on a paper towel, then dab it on your neck, hands and clothing and hunting boots. Pro-Cover works effectively for about five hours.

ITEM: *rubber boots*

Rubber boots keep your feet dry because they don't allow the water to leak in. But most definitely you can reduce your scent trail considerably if you wear rubber boots to and from your hunting blind. Hip boots are most desirable. The right kind are not noisy and heavy. 16" rubber boots would be good. Hunting boots with rubber bottoms are satisfactory—Bean's Maine Hunting Shoe—and are probably what you must wear when still-hunting. Sneakers and leather boots, although they keep your feet cool, let out too much of your scent.

Everyone has smelly feet. All animals have smelly feet. Smell your dog's feet, your cat's feet, and your own feet—if you are flexible enough. If you kill a bear, smell its feet. Catch a chicken and smell the feet. When feet touch the ground they leave the odor of their owners.

ITEM: *duct tape*

The most effective and most odorless insect repellent I know of—Ben's 100—has a slight odor to my nose, and I'm quite sure a black bear could detect that odor and associate it with human proximity. All the other insect repellents are pleasantly scented to make them pleasant to use and may be fine for fishermen, but not for bear hunters. The only insect repellent that should be used in extreme situations—when you're going crazy because you think you're being eaten alive—is Ben's 100. Unfortunately the catch of being squeaky clean and odorless is that is when the bugs—especially blackflies—like you the best. Dirty, smelly people they show less desire for.

The solution to the problem involves the use of duct tape.

First of all, you tuck your headnet down under your shirt. The headnet should be bloused away from the face, otherwise mosquitoes will be able to feed on you through the holes. (Dark green headnets are easier to see through than camo headnets.) Then you put on your camo coveralls. Coveralls, because they are one-piece, permit more convenient bug protection than anything two-piece. Blackfly bites around the belt line are especially annoying, mostly because these are easiest to scratch, and the more you scratch them, the more they itch. With coveralls you'll get less bites around the middle. Then you put on a pair of cotton gloves and have a buddy seal you up with duct tape—around the neck and shoulders to seal the headnet to the collar of your coveralls; around the wrists to seal the gloves to the sleeves; and around the ankles to seal the cuffs to your rubber boots. Then you put on another pair of cotton gloves. Usually mosquitoes can bite through one pair of cotton gloves, but not through two pairs.

Many people become hysterical simply because bugs are flying around them, but not necessarily biting them. You will just have to get used to that. However, if worse comes to worse—some people are allergic to blackfly bites, experiencing fever and nausea and swelling—then you will have no choice but to use a good insect repellent.

Courtesy of the Maine Fish and Game Department.

Photo by Ken Gray.

BEAR & MOOSE

BEAR & MOOSE

Courtesy of Maine Fish and Game Department.

Photos by Tom Carbone.

Courtesy of the Maine Fish and Game Department.

Photo by Ken Gray.

BEAR & MOOSE

Courtesy of the Quebec Ministry of Hunting and Fishing.

Photo by Pierre Bernier.

Courtesy of the Maine Fish and Game Department.

Photo by Bill Gross.

ITEM: *a supply of attracting scent*

I have developed my own attracting scent for bear hunting. It works awful cunning on bruin. He comes in just a trotting and a drooling. Of course the ingredients are a secret. You don't think I'm a fool, do you? Taking a sniff of it, however, you might conclude that my scent for bear hunting is a mixture of oil of anise, liquid smoke, and pure vanilla extract. The directions on the bottles that I hand out to hunters state the following directions: "Store only between 50 F–125 F or 10 C–52 C. Shake well before using. Squirt small amount onto clean scent rag about 20 yds or 18 m upwind of blind. Avoid getting this scent on skin or clothes." My wife brews up a kettle of this attracting scent every spring and fall outside down by the chicken house and demands payment for her services rendered. I charge hunters $5.00 per bottle, which seems more or less to cover my costs.

Also, Tink Nathan has come up with a very interesting attracting scent for bear hunting—Black Bear Scent #7. "It is urine from an old boar and other secret goodies," says Tink. "Urine from a boar brings out the competitive instinct in other boars. Used around a bait station, #7 stimulates these other boars to hit early when you want them to hit. It keeps away the female bears with cubs and small, non-trophy bears."

I haven't tested #7, but Tink tells me that Darryl Lamb, a bowhunter from Maine whom I know, bagged the only two bears in a New Brunswick bear camp of ten hunters, and he was the only one using this particular attracting scent.

CHAPTER 8

Other items of equipment . . . and what happens when the bear isn't at the end of the string?

A BEAR can be harder to find after being hit by an arrow or a bullet than any other big game animal. Fur and fat plug up the hole made by your arrow or bullet. Also a handful of fur absorbs blood like a wick absorbs oil. Consequently very often the blood-trail does not commence immediately and too often the blood-trail is non-existent. So what do you do?

ITEM: *for archers—tracking string*

Ted Lawson of Oregon, Illinois, is credited with the invention of tracking string. Refinements on his original concept are still being designed, most notably by The Game Tracker, Inc., a company based in Flushing, Michigan. Their device is a canister containing a spool of white nylon line—22 or 17-lb. test, 1500 or 2500-ft. long—which attaches to the belly of your bow. You pull the end of the string out through the canister and tie it to your arrow just behind the broadhead.

I first learned of tracking string from an article Lawson wrote in a 1973 issue of *Bowhunter Magazine*. "My bow is a Super Kodiak that draws 68 pounds with a 29¹/2-inch arrow," Lawson explained. "I use homemade arrows of wood and prefer Black Diamond four-blade broadheads for bear . . . . I shoot string. This is a bottle of 30-pound test nylon, center wound. It has no drag on an arrow for about 50 yards of flight. This string is a product used by electricians as a pilot line to pull wire through thin-wall pipe. It is very strong and comes in 400 yard spools. I fasten this bottle to my bow and tie and tape the string just behind the broadhead. When a hit is made the arrow usually breaks off, but the bear pulls out line like a big fish. This is a tremendous help in finding your bear in heavy brush . . . . My hunting partners and I have used this method with great success. It is a million-dollar feeling to pull the string and when nothing jerks back, follow the line knowing the bear is dead. You will find this is especially true after dark when on hands and knees crawling down a bear path."

I experimented with string for a few spring bear seasons but couldn't get it to work nearly as well as Lawson claimed until 1979 when I tried The Game Tracker device. That worked very nicely.

George Webber, of Babylon, New York, a bowhunter of considerable experience, wrote an article in a 1981 issue of *Precision News* about tracking string and hunting bear. Although what Webber said was shamelessly promotional of N——, here is his article:

As time passed, I could feel excitement growing. I knew that this evening would be the evening. So at 8 P.M., still well before dusk—dusk is when I would normally expect to see big game—I was sitting perfectly still on the horizontals of my tree-blind, my bow in my hand, my knuckles paling with tension. As if on cue, with a kind of instinct a hunter has, I looked down and to my left.

At that moment a bear was stepping into view and into the clearing in front of where the grain sack hung. If you can imagine what the smell of bacon and eggs and hot biscuits can do to your stomach juices on mornings when you are especially hungry—then that is what the smell of spoiled beef and pork, dripping with honey and maggots, can do to a bear's sensibilities on evenings when it is hungry.

I couldn't believe my eyes as I felt the rush of adrenalin.

My first contact with N—— was in 1976, when I read a spring bear story he had written. That story aroused my curiosity to the point that I immediately booked a hunt (which ended with me getting a bear) the last week of June, 1977. I hunted again with N—— in 1979 and 1980.

This particular week of June, N—— had four archers hunting out of his bear camp; Bill Ellis and Morrie Wheeler both of Hoosick Falls, N.Y., Bob Wright of Brewster, N.Y., and myself of Babylon, N.Y. Bob and I are good friends, both of us are Shaklee distributors, and since I had my son with me, he brought his son along too. All because N—— had said he would have his son, Peter, this last week of June with him in camp. I suppose Peter was to learn the ropes of the guiding business. Anyway, the three boys were only around ten years of age, all of them, so I brought my wife with me as a babysitter. N—— didn't seem to mind a woman around camp—actually earlier in the spring he had guided two female bowhunters and both had taken good bears.

All four hunting archers this week were shooting PSE equipment; Bob and I 70 lb. Citations, Morrie and Bill 60 lb. Pacers. Being a PSE dealer, I was pleased, of course. Also, at the target butts, from the practice blinds, N—— was showing us his style with his Laser and showing us too, that shooting The Game Tracker didn't affect broadhead flight one bit. I must say I appreciated his demonstrations. I had never considered shooting string before.

N——'s camp is located on Lower Ox Brook Lake in eastern Maine, and is virtually surrounded by some of the best smallmouth bass lakes in the country. For this reason we brought our canoes and fishing tackle. In the mornings we fished such lakes as West Grand, Pug, Scraggly, and Big Lake.

But hunting is what we came for and the best time for bear hunting over bait is in the evening. N—— said we could try it in the morning, and some of us intended to try it, but for various reasons getting out of bed early enough proved to be difficult. Oh, so much easier to go bass fishing early in the morning than it is to go bear hunting at that time!

Adrenalin causes the heart to beat faster. Adrenalin readies the body for an encounter that is about to take place.

In the clearing, the bear began to walk forward toward the bait. It stopped short however, possibly due to an instinct for danger, but presenting me with a going away shot at a slight angle. I had my Citation at full draw and was trying to steady the red dot of my lighted sight pin on a spot directly behind the bear's right shoulder. Should I wait for a better angle? Would the bear spook? Maybe and perhaps. N—— had said to take our best and first good opportunity, because bears have a habit of disappearing as fast and mysteriously as they appear.

The arrow stuck exactly where I had aimed. The sport now changed from hunting to a feeling of fishing. As the line peeled off the spool I was very much reminded of shark fishing, when a shark picks up the mackerel bait and runs with it. I had a feeling I should set the hook. It was exciting; you couldn't see or hear the bear, but there was the string, zinging out of the spool.

Obviously the bear was running fast—somewhere. Then the bear must be slowing to a trot. Then to a walk. The string stopped. It lay there, inert, like a laundry line, from my bow to a tree, to another tree, to a rock—and I could imagine the bear go down. But no! The string began to twitch, and then to tighten. Slowly it began to come off the spool stopping and starting again and again. Finally it hung limply from my bow, never to move, like the laundry line once more.

I had mixed emotions as I searched the ground with my eyes from the tree blind. I spotted my arrow stuck in the ground. Obviously a passthrough—but I had that feeling I had not made a perfect shot. The angle had been too acute, perhaps, and the arrow had entered too far forward, maybe.

As I thought about these dismal possibilities, the sky had turned black, the temperature had dropped, and thunder could be heard off in the distance. Inevitable—in lieu of the unusual heat and humidity of the past few days. However, rain can be the ruination of a blood trail and I was thankful that I had been shooting string that evening. I felt confident. Let it rain like the dickens.

Luckily, though, the rain never came until the wee hours of the morning. Back at camp, the boys were making a fuss so they could come with us and watch us pick up the bear. Fortunately my wife refused to be left alone, and N——just shook his head, very negatively. "No kids in the woods at night. You never know what you can expect. We might be in for a long walk, and someone has to carry the bear and then who is going to carry the kids? The boys will stay here to protect George's wife. Right boys?"

"Oh, gee!" "We never get to go anywhere!" "Dad, you promised!"

Anyway, the four hunters, plus N——, started trailing my bear following the string, propane lights ablaze in the spooky Maine woods.

We proceeded along, everyone quite confident we would find the bear deceased at the end of the string. N——

wisely paid heed to his compass while I led the lantern brigade because at the end of the string there wasn't any dead bear. There was only thunder, lightning, and the beginnings of a blood trail.

We were surprised, of course, that there was no bear at the end of the string, but our expectations were still satisfactory because of the blood-trail. N—— paid more heed to his compass now.

The blood led us for perhaps a good half-mile deeper into the woods. Next to some large boulders we found evidence that the bear had bedded down. The sign indicated that the bear had thrashed around quite a bit before continuing on, downhill now, more than 200 yards to a little spring hole on the side of a ridge. The blood was miniscule where the bear entered the pool and nonexistent where the bear exited from the pool. But we found drops of water on leaves that dripped off the bear.

But no blood. And were the drops of water on the leaves really from the bear? I felt we had been discussing various possibilities endlessly when N—— suddenly and casually said, pointing, "There would be a great place for the bear to die." He was indicating a big blow-down tree about ten yards from the little spring hole.

I flashed my lantern in the direction of the blown down tree and noticed something quite black underneath it. I cautiously stepped a little closer and to my surprise discovered the bear.

We went through a backslapping and handshaking routine. The bear wasn't as large as the nice boar Ellis had downed with his Pacer just the evening before; or obviously as big as the bear Wright kept seeing rubbing its butt on a thick cedar growing between two white birches ten yards from his blind; or obviously as big (if the diameter of droppings means anything) as the huge bear feeding at Wheeler's bait late every night. But my bear weighed on the scales later almost 150 pounds. And the hide was perfect.

And sometimes you don't find the bear at the end of The Game Tracker string, so in the old, time-honored manner, you follow the blood trail.

N—— said he hadn't tracked a bear any longer distance than this before. And if finding my bear was no easy task, getting it out of the woods was no easy task either. All of us, except N——, stood around scratching our heads (and the bug bites) wondering where the dickens we were.

"Please have faith in my compass," N—— said. Which is exactly what we did.

ITEM: *A game carrying device*

A bear when it's dead is quite relaxed, and if you find it soon enough before rigor mortis has occurred, you will have a problem getting it out of the woods. This is because a bear must be carried, not dragged. I have dragged numerous deer out of the woods without any damage at all to their hides. To drag a bear out, however, will almost certainly cause damage to its pelt. If you pay $600 to $1000 for a bear hunt and you bag a good bear then the value of its hide after taxidermy might be $600 to $1000. So you don't want to mess up your investment by dragging it.

There are options. First of all, you can field-dress the bear where you find him and then hang him up overnight if the weather is cool. The weather is seldom cool enough, however, to avoid some spoilage of the meat. But the next day, when the bear is cool and stiff, you can tie him to a pole and two or four or six of you can carry him out of the woods. The hide will still be fine, but you have lost the opportunity of enjoying bear meat at its very best.

The second option is to field-dress the bear and skin him out also right on the spot. Then two, four, or six of you carry out the parts. In Maine, however, this isn't quite legal because they want to see the whole bear at the tagging station.

The third option is to tie the quite relaxed bear to a large pole and try to carry him out to a spot where you can neatly field-dress, skin, and butcher him. The only problem with this is keeping the heavy, relaxed bear tied to the pole. My experiences with this method have been exasperating, because a bear leg will inevitably come untied or a mid portion of the bear come untied and commence swaying and dragging.

The fourth option is a big improvement. You obtain a two-man game carrying device. This is not the aforementioned large pole but something fabricated from strong aluminum tubing, nylon belts and straps, and a 20-inch bicycle wheel. In theory, at least, two men can carry out a 600-lb black bear with this, laughing all the way, without feeling that the task was one of back-breaking drudgery. The problem here will be getting the bear onto the device. Dead, relaxed, 600-lb bears don't roll any easier than they carry. I suggest that you can use two large poles as levers. Anyway, such an intelligent game-carrying device is manufactured and sold by Warren & Sweat of Grand Island, Florida. I actually bought one from them using a credit card.

The fifth option is the best. This is a transporting device made from thick, slick, flexible plastic with rope and straps. Originally designed for securing and dragging injured mountaineers over snow, it works just fine for tugging—by means of four people—a weighty bear around trees and over rocks and bushes. It is available from Old Jake Products of Paulet, Vermont.

ITEM: *A game dressing kit*

Whether you dress and butcher your bear before or after you get him out of the woods you should be sufficiently organized ahead of time with all the implements required secured in a bag or knapsack or packbasket. It's so much easier when someone shoots a bear to grab the bag with the dressing kit instead of several people searching around camp for all the items needed—and, of course, not being able to find everything.

Although I have a special packbasket containing my dressing kit, probably a carry-bag with a full-length zipper would be more convenient for storing and transporting all the items. Anyway, the bag should contain the following: a gambrel of lightweight, durable steel, tested to 750 pounds, that can hold the bear by one leg or two; a hoist with a 7 to 1 lifting ratio—makes 175 pounds lift like 25—with 65 feet of cord; a bone saw; and a washable, reusable game bag that can protect the bear-carcass from maggot-flies. Walpro Sporting Equipment of Auburn, Alabama, sells such a kit, if you don't want to be bothered assembling one yourself.

ITEM: *A survival kit*

Every hunter should have a survival kit as part of his gear— and have it with him whenever he goes into the woods of the Northeast Wilderness.

My survival kit consists of the following: spare compass; spare knife; spare eyeglasses; spare bootlaces; spare flashlight (a penlight is good enough); two or more fire-starting systems (a butane lighter, steel wool, and water-proofed matches; wax-soaked cardboards and a wax-soaked match-bundle); whistle (the shrill sound of it probably scares coyotes, I hope); space blanket; 3' X 3' folded, heavy-duty aluminum foil (useful for signaling, reflecting heat, making a drinking cup, etc.); first aid items (iodine, Band-aids, aspirin); 25' nylon rope; and a chocolate bar. My brand is Cadbury.

CHAPTER 9

An early experience I had hunting black bear

ONCE I was on the back of a large, live black bear. The position was precarious, and I didn't remain for long that way, and the whole situation was an accident, but I actually have ridden a bear. And I was actually hunting a bear. No one bear in particular. Any bear.

Two friends were with me—not at the moment I was riding, but at my side soon afterwards to observe the circumstantial evidence. They were hunting any bears also.

Well, any bears except very, very small ones or female bears. How you can tell a female bear from a male bear unless you get up really close for a look or a feel is beyond my powers of discernment, and I am familiar with sexual differences. I used to think, when observed distantly, male bears had a general air of macho about them. And female bears acted dainty. That was my rule of thumb for guessing sex. My records proved I was 19% correct.

My two friends are highly placed now in the guiding hierarchy of Maine. Today they are careful about their reputations. When it happened—my riding a bear—I could have had them sign an affidavit for me, but now that would be as hard as getting the Joint Chiefs of Staff to testify before Congress that they believe in UFOs. So I won't use these

84

friends' real names. Instead I'll call them "Aristotle" and "Plato."

"Iss there where it happened?" Plato asked skeptically, smiling at me. His false teeth were back at camp in a glass of water—so he showed mostly gums.

"There's apple trees down below there," Aristotle observed. His knowledge of horticulture and his ability to classify species of flora seemed amazing to me although I think at the time I must have been particularly ignorant. Aristotle was drinking (yes, boozing as we were hunting) and was stumbling. He'd poked Plato twice with a broadhead—the day before yesterday and yesterday.

In those days Aristotle's favorite beverage came in a uniquely shaped bottle. He flaunted his proclivity for that brand of booze. His mother (blessed woman) even fashioned a leather holster so her boy could wear it on his gun belt. His .44 hung on his right hip and his favorite booze on his left. Quite a sight and everyone in Aristotle's social circle was impressed. Now he is a teetotaler having discerned, contrary to his expectation and hope, that alcohol and profit in the guiding business don't mix.

Aristotle smoked a pipe, and Plato and I followed him, stomping out the fires he started.

"Ah, here are some old bear droppings," I said.

"Oh, yeah," Aristotle said.

"Yess," Plato said.

"With chokecherries," Aristotle noted. "See the seeds. There's bear in here." He poked at the droppings with an arrow. We had our bows and arrows. Those were the days of finely crafted, heavy recurves. In fact, when his recurve was new and fresh, Plato took it to bed with him. Plato has a fetish like that, you might say. Sort of a holdover from his childhood. He took his stuffed dog to bed, when it was new. Then his first Donald Duck toothbrush. Then an electric wall clock, a birthday present, which short-circuited and had to be returned. And most recently he's having a fling with a turbocharged 4X4. How about that? Well, I imagine it takes up most of the space. I mean, he hardly has room for his new cam bow.

"Don't you use an insert with your broadheads?" I asked Aristotle.

"I have some with it and some without it," he replied, flaming cinders erupting from his pipe. Plato and I stomped them out.

"Here iss more droppings!" Plato shouted.

"What's in them?" Aristotle asked.

"More seeds! And here iss a worn path!"

Plato was excited. He waved his arms, and because Aristotle had swayed close to Plato to contemplate the worn path indicated, his pipe was knocked from his mouth. It flew into a taxus canadensis and instantly started a fire.

Immediately I jumped onto the prickly bush into the flames and did a dance. I extinguished the fire and managed to break Aristotle's pipe.

"Fletching cement might fix it," Aristotle muttered, receiving from me the three pieces of his pipe and quick-drawing his bottle.

"I was up this tree over the path," I said, getting back to business.

"Yess," Plato said, smiling at me.

"Oh, yeah," Aristotle said, gulping.

"See the broken limb," I said. The broken white cedar limb was obvious, so I didn't point at it.

"Where?"

"Where?"

So I pointed at the broken limb and explained again exactly what had happened. Nothing about my bear ride was complicated or hard to understand. It had been just an accident—an accident that resulted in my riding a bear, holding tight to its neck. Undoubtedly I had ridden with the wild hope in mind that I could choke the beast to death or at least limit its air supply to slow it—so I could dismount gracefully. And if not exactly gracefully, at least dismount uninjured.

I believe my friends understood. Aristotle quick-drew his bottle, splashing me with whiskey. I think he even considered offering me a drink—his eyes had a momentary glaze—but he succumbed to stronger feelings and took gulps himself. Plato tried not to smile—a positive sign of his comprehension. He is usually smiling.

Anyway, today's archers with compound bows have a certain advantage that we didn't have with recurves. Because of their short length—about fifty inches long—compounds are more maneuverable than recurves in tight situations. And trees overlooking worn game paths usually make for tight situations. My bow then was a 58-pound Super Kodiak, 64 inches long. That's a pretty long recurve.

An archer I know from Massachusetts says he sometimes shoots at game using his feet—that is, he holds the bow out horizontally with his feet, and then lets loose arrows. "Sometimes it's the only way possible," he says.

The only way possible in this situation I decided was with my feet, unless . . . unless the bear passed into a particular opening about ten yards up the path from where I was tangled in the white cedar tree. Otherwise my elbows had nowhere to go and upper bow-limb would smash against a branch and lower bow-limb possibly alter my anatomy. I rejected the feet-idea, because I hadn't practiced it ever and sensibly opted for the small opening I could see at ten yards. I planned to draw back my arrow if the bear walked under me on the path and hold until the bear reached the opening. Then I was going to give it to the bear good.

I had found the bear's droppings, the apple trees, the path and the tree by the path by about 4:00. Two hours later my buttocks were sore and my legs numb because of the cramped position I had been obliged to assume in the tree. I had stood for a while, had leaned for a time, had sat for intervals—however, a thick branch might seem comfortable at first but as the minutes tick away you discover that impression isn't accurate.

Suddenly—while my legs were tingling and demanding of me where their feelings had gone—the bear was right under me. My discomforts were forgotten.

I drew back my arrow, but the bear remained under the tree.

Remember, my bow was a recurve, 58 pounds.

Another advantage of a compound is that you can hold it longer. Say, if my bow had been a 58-pound compound, with a 50% relaxation, then even my grandmother could have held it. Yes, Grandma could hold 29 pounds—provided, of course, I helped her yank past the hump—the initial peak-weight of 58 pounds. I imagine Grandma could hold 29 pounds indefinitely.

Black bears vocalize extensively. This is surprising because bears are not social as are most primates and some of the big cats and wolves. This doesn't mean they vocalize to themselves out of boredom or loneliness, however. "Not social" doesn't mean, for example, that bears have mating experiences devoid of romance. They do and they don't. As a matter of fact, somewhere in the literature I've collected on black bears is a reference to I.Q. tests administered to the creatures—much of it in mating situations. The tester concluded that the testees had high intelligence, possibly the highest of all four-legged beasts, which would include the big cats and wolves. (People and monkeys are primates. You may conclude, therefore, that Plato and Aristotle and all the monkeys are smarter than the average bear. I mean, you really can't escape that conclusion.)

Anyway, my black bear was saying something to itself. It was sniffing around the base of my tree, and woofing. "Woof," it said. Evidently, the furry thing had detected my scent and wasn't too happy about it.

I was still holding, at full draw, a 29-inch, 2020 aluminum arrow quivering on my 58-pound recurve. The bear stayed under the tree.

At the time if I suspected compounds were not going to be invented, I would have invented one there. With great stealth and quiet, I would have hacked off lengths from each recurved limb, screwed on wheels rigged with cables, made adjustments to the bowstring, etc., and then maybe I would have been able to bend and shoot directly down. Certainly I couldn't do this with that long recurve.

The bear was still woofing. "Woof!" it said, again, perhaps for the tenth time.

In those days when I bowhunted I wore sneakers, and sometimes heavy socks over the sneakers, and in the fall (September is fall in Maine) I would saturate the sneakers and the socks with deer scent so that by the time archery season for deer came around in October my sneakers and all my socks (the ones worn under, too, not to mention my feet) would be good and stinky. The scent cost me $4.99 a tiny bottle from Keith-the-Thief, owner of my local archery equipment store, which was open evenings, Monday, Wednesday, and Friday. Tuesday, Thursday, and Saturday evenings, according to the rumors, Keith-the-Thief drove his rusted Jap pickup to the airport to give his money to a pilot he knew who flew it to a bank in Switzerland. So that's why his archery store wasn't open those evenings. Sundays, Keith visited archery tournaments, selling his scent and other items out of the back of his pickup—and when he wasn't at the tournaments he was out stalking his pet deer (he kept seven) with a funnel and hundreds of empty, tiny bottles. His scent was very popular and Keith promoted it well—sending free samples to outdoor writers, outdoor-magazine editors, etc.

Obviously, Keith-the-Thief's scent on my sneakers was what the bear was sniffing.

A bear's keenest sense is its sense of smell. Its ability to see is poor, and its ability to hear is only fair. A bear can detect movement, though perhaps not as quickly as a deer. I have found it far more difficult from a blind to take pictures of deer than of bear. Even Keith-the-Thief has great difficulty, he says, collecting his scent from his pet deer. He has to be totally camouflaged to resemble as nearly as possible another deer or perhaps one of his neighbor's Jersey cows—with which, he says, his pet deer have a friendly relationship.

A bear is not especially alarmed by the clicking of a shutter or even flashes of light. I remember, for example, Grandma taking pictures once of bears with an instamatic and flashcubes. The dump supervisor, a hippy with sunglasses, had just handed out to the bears bottles of carbonated colas or something, and the bears were gulping these down, and not in the least bit distracted by Grandma's efforts at close-up picture taking.

Surely a bear can hear a camera ten yards away. My theory is a bear is smart enough not to give a damn if his picture is being taken. He thinks it doesn't hurt, so what's the big deal.

But when a heavy aluminum hunting arrow (with a broadhead that's sharp enough to shave the fuzz off a porcupine's nose) starts to rattle against the sight window of a 58-pound hunting bow, a bear hears the rattle and starts to move away fast.

My arrow started to rattle against my bow. My strength, and my ability to hold, were fading fast.

"Woof," the bear said. "Woowoowoo."

Suddenly that particular limb of the white cedar, where I sat, broke. The arrow flew off, and my bow and I came tumbling down, precisely straddling the back of the bear. The bear's four legs were in motion, but the bear himself had not moved—that is, he had not overcome inertia. Not quite. Obviously I had overcome inertia faster than he had. Hard to explain.

And difficult to judge under such circumstances the actual size of a bear. But I fit well on his back and my feet didn't drag on the ground. His fur was thick, though not especially long. To hold on I had to grab the fur on the bear's neck. I had to drop my bow, of course.

"How did you get off him?" Aristotle asked.

"I can't say exactly," I said.

"Dist you hurt your bow?" Plato asked.

I inspected my bow. There was dry blood on it from my nose. The only noteworthy injury to anything had been to my nose. So I was having trouble breathing, and I'd lost the arrow.

"The bow is okay," I said.

"You have to be careful sitting in a white cedar tree," Aristotle noted. He staggered, poking Plato with a broadhead.

I got out a Band-aid and we were all very matter-of-fact. But I could tell that Plato and Aristotle wished they had had my experiences—although Plato has recently developed a good moose story he tells mostly at meetings of the guides' association and Aristotle has come up with a rather exciting deer yarn he unwinds when he has milk and cookies with his hunting clients.

CHAPTER 10

Some of the experiences people tell you they have had with black bears should be appreciated as works of art, not of truth.

A GOOD story is often only a good story. But that's okay. The fables of the Northeast Wilderness are many and worthy. I remember a trip to the Nepisiguit River near Bathurst, New Brunswick, one August. I was flyfishing for Atlantic Salmon. One evening the Licensed Outfitter, Kenneth Gray, introduced me to his father, George, who told us a good bear story. He swears it is completely true. However, I feel fortunate that I had remembered purchasing a bottle of whiskey at the tax-free shop in Calais, Maine. Any attempts I have made to correct the grammar fault the tone too much. What you read is what I heard on my tape recorder.

"When I was about sixteen, my oldest brother says to me he's going up river to trap bears. I had never seen bears trapped. My brother had five big bear traps that weighed each one about forty pounds. He had trapped quite a few springs up river and where we was going was all lumber camps. The camps was half a mile apart on a road by the river, and in the spring after they had cut all winter, the logs would go into the river, this river here, and be moved to the mill. And there was a certain time in the spring when there was nobody in the camps at all. Of course at every one of the camps there would be a dumping place where they would throw the old potatoes, the old meat, and the trash. And on the road, from the first camp right up to the last camp—I think it was about three miles—there was nothing but bear tracks.

"It took my brother and me three days to get there. We had a great big dog with us, a mongrel breed, that wouldn't back away from anything. We thought she would tackle a bear. She weighed about 90 pounds and my brother didn't like her in the canoe. We poled the canoe from here where we sit now drinking whiskey right clean up three days. That's fifty-six miles. And we put out the bear traps. First we would get some bait—porcupines or rabbits—and then build houses for the traps and set them and cover them with leaves. We only had one gun—a .35 Remington with the pump underneath. And we had the axe. We stayed at night in a shelter made with boughs. One night at about twelve o'clock we hear the most ungodly yelps that I ever heard before in the woods. We had never before seen that dog get scared, but her tail went right in between her two legs and she started to shiver. She came right between me and my brother and lay on the blankets. Sometimes the ungodly yelps were pretty loud so I knew something was handy. My brother says, 'It must be bears fighting.' I started to shiver like the dog and never slept a wink the rest of that night.

"After a couple of days—we're also trapping muskrats and beaver—my brother says to me that the next morning we're to see if we got a bear. He said, 'We must have a bear with all them signs.'

"In the morning we start with a lunch in our packs following the old trail—the three-mile road—which followed the river quite handy. The dog is in between us and we're tripping over her. Because we had gales of wind near the river the leaves was off the first trap and my brother stopped to fix it. I grabbed the rifle and walked ahead to see another trap. The dog followed me. That time the porcupines was awful in New Brunswick. They would get in the traps and then you would have to reset the traps, but one person couldn't do it alone. Them were big traps. But we went along that way seeing the traps, me ahead of my brother, catching nothing so far except for a few porcupines.

"I am getting anxious so I says to my brother, 'I'm going to run to the last trap. If we have a bear, I'll run right back.' I leave the rifle with my brother. The dog knows enough to stay where the rifle is. I start running, and I went about two or three-hundred yards when I hear on the side of the trail a stick break . . . crack! I stop. I look. I don't see a damn thing. So I start walking, and I'm thinking about them awful yelps we heard that made the dog nervous. I'm a little nervous. I look behind me a couple of times. I don't see nothing. About the third time I look behind, there's a bear on the road, a great big bear about . . . that high. It is heading where I am going. Right then I have in mind if I could pass that last trap and there's nothing in it, that bear is going to get caught in that trap. So I start to walk pretty damn fast and I look behind. Gee, the bear is coming like hell, too. And I'm coming to a turn in the road. When I get around the turn, and I can't see the bear, I run as fast as I can so I can pass that trap! Hell, at that time I could run. So I run for about a minute and I look behind, and gee, the bear is coming too.

"The bear is no further behind me than fifty feet. And I know then that I couldn't pass the trap. Right away I say to myself, 'That bear is after me.' So I start to look ahead while I'm running to see if I can find a tree with boughs handy to the ground. Sure enough I only went another fifty feet or so and, gee, there's a great big spruce tree near the road with big boughs. I am played out then, and I hit that tree half falling, but as quick as I can I climb twenty feet. That bear comes along and goes right by. Never stops. Gee, I'm looking at where the bear went and I see the bear coming back toward the tree! Right near the foot of the tree! It starts to smell around on the ground. Then it smells up the tree. Gee! It starts to climb!

"Now, right in back of this spruce there is a rotten pine, big and round, that had broke off nice and even twenty feet up. I say to myself, 'I wonder if I can hide behind that pine.' Some dead branches of the pine are in among the boughs of the spruce and that spruce is starting to shake! So I step along on the dead branches and reach that pine, and gee, the pine is hollow!

"I think to myself that the bear will never find me down in that hole, so down I go, hanging on the rim with my hands and with my feet braced. From inside the pine I can see the top of the spruce moving. And then . . . next damn thing I see is two paws about this size . . . right near my hands. I let go. I fall right down inside the rotten pine, bing, bang, about twenty feet. But I fall on something not too hard . . . didn't hurt me. And I could see the daylight at the rim . . . the paws and arms coming over. And then the hole gets black and dirt starts coming down, sticks falling in my eyes. I can't see no more daylight.

"The only thing I have is my jackknife. I have no hunting knife. And the big blade on that jackknife isn't too big.

I know the bear would be coming down backwards. So I get my knife out and open up the biggest blade. I put up my left hand . . . like that . . . and when I feel the fur of the bear I grab it and hold on tight and with my right hand I up with the blade of that knife. I feel the hot blood hit me in the face. And that bear makes a jump for the top and at the same time I'm hanging on. I up with the knife again and the bear makes another jump. I up again and again. Finally we make it to the rim of the pine and the bear jumps down for the road, never minding the spruce tree at all. But when the bear jumps it hits its head on a rock and never moves.

"So I come down, all covered with blood. It seems to me the bear killed itself right there. I have my jackknife and I start skinning. I skin, skin, and get the skin off, and wrap it up, put it in my little pack, and I start back to see my brother. I meet him coming up with the gun, the axe, and the dog. He says, 'I think you had a long lunch. Why are you covered with blood?' I says, 'I killed a bear.' He says, 'How could you kill a bear? I got the gun.' I says, 'The bear must have killed itself.' So then we get in an argument because he says a bear don't kill itself and he thinks I killed the bear when it was in the trap. He says, 'A jackknife isn't enough. You need a gun.' I says, 'I didn't even go to the trap. The bear is around the turn. It's a big bear.'

"So we start walking to where I skinned the bear. My brother is excited and we keep tripping over the dog. When we get there, there is no bear. My brother says, 'The bear just stunned itself. You skinned it while it was unconscious. When it come to, it walked away.'

"Well, in a few days we catch a bear in a trap that is the funniest bear ever seen. It has a skin just like a pig. No hair on the sides at all. Only a few little hairs on the back. My brother says, 'That's the same bear that you skinned and that walked away.' So as soon as we can we go back to that old pine that is hollow. My brother and I are sitting there with the dog, my brother smoking his pipe, and I am telling over again everything that happened when all of a sudden we hear a noise. It's in the pine. Something like scratching. Something going . . . grarr, grarr, grarr . . . . My brother says, 'Gee, what's that?' I says, 'Something that followed the blood is down there.' So my brother hands me the rifle and takes the axe and starts cutting a great big notch into the hollow pine. Two little bears is there! That was a she I skinned and that big pine was the den with her cubs. When I fell in the hollow pine, that is why it was soft when I hit bottom! The she-bear was following me to her den to protect her two little ones. I feel bad and my brother is mad at me. But we feel good when it looks like the dog is adopting the little bears or the other way around. The dog growls but the cubs keep looking for her milk. They won't leave her alone.

"We took the little bears down river with us and my brother and I fed them until they were big. When the bears got big they started into fighting. The yelps they made were just like those ungodly yelps that I heard before in the woods. The dog didn't like anything about the bears when they got big so in the fall at first snow around November we took them back up river."

CHAPTER 11

*Fall is the best season of the year for black-bear action hunting.
Not black-bear trophy hunting—although that could happen,
too. Bryce Towsley, a writer and my friend, will explain about
this in the following narrative, which originally appeared in a
1985 issue of* The Vermont Sportsman.

THE story here has a title which indicates that it's about
handgunning black bears. I have performed just some minor
editing. Bryce spells worse than I do. He also writes
uniquely. I gave up trying to correct everything. I have
removed all shamelessly promotional references, however,
by means of—

When I think of a bear guide I picture a big man, barrel
chested, with a wild beard and arms like virgin timber. A
man that likes his whiskey straight, fights his bears bare
handed and loves his women wild.

So when I spotted N——'s name tag at the New England Outdoor Writers annual meeting I was sure that there
was a mix-up. I knew N—— from some brief correspondence and through mutual friends, but the man with the
tag couldn't be a bear guide. The image that came to mind
was "orthopedic surgeon," not "bear guide." This man was
slight of build with glasses, prematurely graying hair and a

look of academia. I was sure that what had happened was the partying got out of hand the night before and this man had N—'s tag as a mistake or maybe to protect the real N—— from some irate husband. I introduced myself, hoping to straighten things out. But there was no mix-up! This studious looking man was indeed a bear guide and the proprietor of Seven Arrows Guiding Service.

I have always thought that when not hunting, bear guides spent their time guzzling whiskey, brawling, and cutting firewood. Once again, N—— shattered my illusions. He spends his time also writing, not only outdoor articles, but novels and poetry. N—— plays tennis, eats healthy foods and drinks only the finest Scotch.

My stereotypes devastated and my mind clawing for some fragment of reality for their salvation, we settled into conversations of bear hunting. I soon learned that N—— was indeed a competent bear hunter. He is concerned not so much with numbers but with quality. As one could surmise from the outfit's name the primary means is with bow and arrow. Purity of sport is imperative as can be seen in N——'s motto: "like the voice of a swallow" (from the *Odyssey*); "ancient and honorable" (from N——). With this in mind I talked to N—— about the ethics and attitudes of handgun hunters and how they parallel those of the bowhunter rather closely. He seemed to think it worth a look and I booked a hunt for the first week of September.

The drive from my house near Rutland, Vt. to the meeting point at the Pine Tree Store in Grand Lake Stream was 445 miles. Much of this was along the rural, two-lane blacktop of Rt. 2. This road winds itself through Maine at a pace that at times seems a decade behind the rest of the world. The houses speak of the poverty of the region. Most yards contain a large woodpile and a couple of junk cars instead of shrubs and a swimming pool. Occasionally you pass a house that, while modest by many standards, beams like a beacon in this region. It leaves you wondering what employment allows the occupants to live at this higher standard. The paper company towns are identified by the stench in the air noticed miles before you reach the town on the downwind side. The houses here denote the obviously higher income of the inhabitants. You think that perhaps the increased income has normalized their culture. But then you notice that the styles of the hair and clothes are a couple of years behind even the urban areas of Vermont, let alone New York. In the fast-food restaurants there is the usual collection of young girls in their late teens and things seem normal, until you notice that more have on wedding rings than don't.

As the road winds through an uninhabited area, the trees growing right to the edge of the road and backed by miles of relatively flat land will stir claustrophobic feelings in a Vermonter used to meadows ending in a mountain. But it also gives you time to think. Driving on, I think that the negative aspects of the lifestyle here are easily observable, but to see the benefits you must seek them out. The people live in a land harsh in climate and economics. They survive and in many ways they prosper. Realizing this suddenly, it seems a better place to live.

But enough of geography and economics—the traffic thins so I crank up some rock-and-roll and slide the pedal down. As the miles melt away behind me, I'm feeling good. The world be damned! I'm going hunting.

I am met at the Pine Tree Store by Harry Vanderweide who informs me that because of some lost luggage belong-

ing to another hunter, N—— was delayed at the Bangor Airport. Harry had directions to N——'s camp, and we headed
for it. We were to stay there as we were a contingent of writers
and N—— thought those lodgings better under the circumstances than to stay in Grand Lake Stream like the other
clients. Later N—— arrived with Bob Knopf who had recovered his luggage and we settled into a dinner of caribou stew.

Harry is the editor of *The Maine Sportsman,* the Maine
editor for *Outdoor Life,* has written a couple of books, appears on an outdoor television show and is a columnist for
a weekly newspaper. Bob is the marketing director for
Berkley fishing-tackle and is a freelance writer/photogra-
pher. Joining us on Tuesday would be Tony Kinton, a Mississippi writer/photographer, and Ben Rogers Lee, who in
turkey and whitetail circles needs no introduction.

I was the only powder-burner in the crowd. I was
shooting a .44 magnum with SSK Industry's 320 gr. cast-
bullets at a chronographed speed of just over 1300 fps. This
bullet has been designed for African game and I was most
interested to see it perform on bear. While testing it at home
before the hunt I was impressed with its striking energy and
with its unreal penetration. I want my animals to have two
holes in their hides from each bullet, one in and one out.
While passing through, I want as much tissue damage as
possible. Because variables like the angle of the shot and the
size of the bear are not controllable, I opt to err on the side
of penetration. Others may theorize that a bullet is at its best
when stopping at the skin on the far side, thereby expending
all its energy in the target. All good in theory, but I don't
buy it. I want my holes punched through and I was confident that this bullet would do it, no matter what part of the
bear it hit.

The gun was a Ruger Super Blackhawk 7^1/$_2$ inch. When I first took it out of the box the trigger pull was so bad that, if pulled slow enough, the sear would not release and the gun wouldn't fire. The pull was tough enough that weight-training was required for the index finger on the shooting hand to avoid cramps when shooting. A couple of hours at the work bench with a stone and a replacement return-spring from Trapper Gun Works got the ugly out and brought the pull to a more reasonable three pounds. Then the damn cylinder wouldn't turn after the first two shots. I relieved the recoil plate where the case heads were binding and finally I had a decent shooter.

I know all about the liability panic that resulted in this kind of trigger, but it seems that most of the corporate lawyers and marketing people are missing the obvious. A lot of shooters won't even buy a gun that needs attention before it is usable but a lot more shooters will try to do the work themselves. I would rather see the factory do it right than some table-top butcher turning out guns that aren't safe. Once the bugs are out, though, the Ruger is about the best .44 on the market. It shoots very well and will last almost forever.

For sighting, I chose an Aimpoint Mark III. For those not familiar, this is an electronic sight that floats a red dot in optical range of the sight. Once adjusted, any time you can see the dot, you put it on the target and pull the trigger. You will hit what you're shooting at! The sight has unlimited eye-relief and no parallax, which solves a lot of problems for a pistol shooter. The model I have has no magnification and I don't think that it's necessary for shots expected when hunting over bait. I believe that for hunting in the forested areas of the northeast, there isn't a better sight going for a handgun. My only complaint is that it is a little big and heavy, which led me away from a holster. Actually, the No. 4 shoulder-holster from Uncle Mike's worked quite well, but I wanted to try a sling and I needed an excuse. I had the grip-frame drilled and tapped to take a swivel on the barrel and added a nylon sling from the same Uncle Mike's. A set of Pachmayer grips completed the rig. The gun sure gets attention wherever it goes. It's also my idea of a hell of a bear-gun.

One of the first rules of successful bear hunting is to remember that a bear's primary defense is his nose. To lure a bear into the ranges that we expected to be shooting at, a hunter must be virtually odor-free. For our clothing that was no problem. Before coming to Maine each of us had carefully washed our hunting togs and stored them in a clean plastic bag. Our bodies were another thing altogether. Each day before hunting they required cleansing. Having SCUBA dived in Maine several times, I was aware that a Mainer's idea of "warm" water was any not in solid form. So when N—— suggested that we swim in the lake to wash up, I had a premonition of what was coming. A Maine lake in September is not my idea of "creature comforts." Had we chosen to stay in town, hot showers would have been available. Instead, we picked N——'s base camp to house us and this was the way it was done there. One must suffer for his art, so each day at two o'clock screams could be heard echoing around the lake as we stripped down and plunged in. We washed every crack and crevice with a product called Sportsman's ODOR AWAY which was supposed to eliminate odors whatever the origin. Apparently it worked.

The first night (Monday) was stagnant. Although we were keyed-up with anticipation, fueled by a bear that was jumped off the bait as N——— and Harry approached Harry's stand, nothing showed.

Tuesday, Harry jumped the same bear off the bait. It seems that the fellow was camping there and had made his bed under the tree-stand. Later, he had a cub feeding at his bait and Momma keeping guard. When they left, the camper came back, but he didn't offer a shot.

Wednesday the camper was back and granted Harry a shot. All the anticipation was too much, though. Harry was nerved-up from all the bears he was seeing and he discovered that a bear is a different target than a bale of hay. Harry, who outshot everyone in the friendly contests at camp, missed.

Thursday Bob had a shot at a small bear that heard him draw and outran the arrow. (Best excuse I've ever come across. Outdoor writers are a creative lot, aren't they?) Actually, the bear turned as he released and the arrow went where the bear used to be. Ben Lee came in and told us he had hit a good bear just before dark. I hadn't seen a thing.

I am by nature not a passive hunter, so sitting on a stand is pure torture. If I fail to mend my ways before I die, the Devil will undoubtedly damn me to sit in an unproductive tree-stand for all eternity. My body is adult in size, geriatric in condition and a toddler in disposition. When ordered to sit still it pleads, pouts, fidgets, throws tantrums, whines, screams, needs a drink and has to go to the bathroom. After hours of sitting still through all this and seeing only the no-see-ums eating my tender skin for wildlife, these tales were too much to bear. The only big game I had seen was a large bull moose that refused me passage on what he claimed as his road. I was not in a mood for negotiations and figured to drive through no matter what the moose thought. But when I narrowed the distance to a few feet and compared his massive size to my mini-pickup, I reconsidered, backed up and waited for him to saunter off.

So as the other hunters all told of bears aplenty I felt a scream welling up, but suppressed it and went to help look for Ben's bear with the rest of the gang.

Without detailing it here, believe me when I say that trailing a wounded bear that ain't happy through the Maine woods after dark armed only with a small pocket knife is exciting stuff. We recovered Ben's bear and believe me again when I tell you that carrying a dead bear two miles through the Maine swamps so as not to mess up the hide is not exciting stuff. It's hard work!

Friday was the last chance. I was in a tree stand absolutely sure that it was all a conspiracy. The gods hated me, my mother-in-law had hired a voodoo man to curse me so I'd quit hunting and take better care of her daughter and her hired krishnas were chanting for the bears. I was certain that Ben had killed the last bear in the state of Maine. In short, I was discouraged. I had ruined many a bird season by spending my time looking for bears. Deer hunting was spent following bear tracks instead of bucks, and still I had no rug on my floor. I was sure this would be the time it was going to happen, but the prospects looked bleak. Like Dylan, I was "tangled up in blue."

It is really amazing how something as simple as a stick breaking can change the condition of the world. If they could bottle that stuff and sell it, it would probably be illegal. The stick in question had cracked behind me ten minutes ago and the rush was deserting me to my previous state of self-pity. I hadn't dared move my head to look and when nothing else happened, my mind started to drift back to all the work that waited at home. It was probably only a squirrel, anyway. Then another stick snapped beside me, ON THE SIDE AWAY FROM THE BAIT. The bear wasn't supposed to be there, but it was. It wasn't planning on staying, though. Something wasn't to its liking and it was departing. When I cocked the big single-action, the noise sent the bear into overdrive. I swung the red dot of the Aimpoint with the black form and pulled the trigger. I wasn't as fast as the bear and I knew as the gun bucked that I was too far back. The bear turned and ran back the way it came, looking like a bowling ball approaching Mach I. I recocked the pistol as I pulled it out of recoil and tried to get the dot on the black blur. The next shot was still echoing through the swamp when the bear disappeared.

I reloaded the two empty chambers with hands that were shaking like a drunk on the wagon and threw down everything that wouldn't break. I'm not sure if I climbed down or jumped, but everything still works, so I guess I used the ladder.

I found blood where I had last seen the bear and started following the trail. The brush was so thick that visibility in places was less than the length of my body and I am not a tall man. Trailing a wounded bear in this kind of territory armed with a handgun had the adrenalin pumping through my arteries like they were fire hoses. It occurred to me that I was all alone, there was no place to run and help was miles away. It just was me and the bear. I would have traded places with anyone in the world at that moment.

The blood-trail was easy to follow as the bullet had done its job well. I followed it through the brush and across the road I had walked in on. I had traveled thirty yards on the other side before I spotted a black form lying in a depression. I could detect no breathing so I advanced slowly and circled, keeping the cocked pistol on the bear until I could touch its eye with a long stick. The eye didn't blink and I knew it was over.

I dragged the bear to the road and walked the mile back to my truck. I could, by moving only a few branches, drive to the bear, load it into the truck and head for N——'s camp.

The bullet had caught the 2^{1}/$_{2}$ year old female on a descending angle at the left hip, exiting out the right side behind the ribs. The exit hole gave me the blood trail necessary to track the bruin the hundred yards it was able to travel. The severe impact of the 320 gr. bullet made sure that, even with a marginal hit, it went only that distance. Not surprisingly, I could find no evidence of the other shot connecting.

I was not the only one to have an active evening. Bob had three bears just out of bow range fighting over some bait they had stolen, when a bigger bear came and ran them off. Tony had been sitting in his tree-stand when it began to shake. He looked down and found himself face to face with a big bear that was halfway up the ladder. The bear found out what it wanted to know and boogied, leaving Tony shaken but excited enough to book for next year as soon as he staggered back to N——'s camp. In all, the week gave us a total of 13 bear sightings. Surely, some were repeats of the same bear, but still not too shabby a week, particularly when I think about my ration of sightings-to-hours-spent here in Vermont.

I have lived and hunted in bear country all my life and for years I've heard that bear meat is best admired at a distance and then given away. That night we barbecued the tenderloin from Ben's bear and I agreed. If you get a bear, give the meat away. I'll take all you've got! Without a doubt, that meat had some flavor enhancement by my elation and the location, but it has yet to be surpassed by any wild game I've eaten.

CHAPTER 12

*I have never hunted black bear with a crossbow, but I can
imagine what it is like, and there are certain problems involved.*

ALL the crossbow hunters I talked with told me they knew
people who had killed deer with crossbow equipment. They
knew of no reason why black bear couldn't be killed the
same way, but they didn't know anybody who had actually
done that deed yet. One contact told me he thought he knew
a fellow who knew a fellow . . . etc.

I made arrangements to hunt Ontario the spring of 1984
with a nationally known outfitter—actually a friend of
mine—who at first said he would be pleased by the publicity I could get him if I were successful, but later phoned me
in a somewhat agitated huff to cancel my hunt: he had been
advised that any story I might write about a crossbow
hunt for black bear, outfitted by him, would be bad for his
business, which is 90% archery oriented. To my knowledge, all the traditional archery organizations and most
archery equipment manufacturers are presently fearful of
the current surge in crossbow interest. They view cross-
bow-archery as a heresy that threatens the foundations of
traditional archery: i.e., special big-game seasons before and
after regular seasons.

Be that as it may, however, this crossbow-threat to my hunting freedoms only makes me yawn. I have been through the dark days of the compound heresy and made it with my freedoms intact. In fact, I have a freedom added. Now I can shoot bows with wheels (or with cams) as well as my longbows and recurves.

I have been hunting black bear since 1968—in Maine until 1981 in the spring and presently in the fall. Also, I hunt black bear in New Brunswick spring and fall. But in neither Maine nor New Brunswick is crossbow hunting legal. It is permitted in Ohio (where bruin does not exist) and Ontario. In any case, I have known people who enjoyed a sporting chase with bows and arrows, muzzleloaders, rifles, and pistols. Once I met a person who had a sincere desire to kill a bear with a spear. I thought he was joking until he showed me his spear. I had no desire to hunt with him and sent him packing. Even though to hunt with a spear is perfectly legal in Maine, this man wished to perform a stunt—which I can't tolerate—rather than engage in sport. I define a stunt as either dangerous to the hunter or cruel to the game or both. For some years I refused to associate with pistol hunters, believing they wished to perform stunts cruel to the game. It took a while, but I have since changed my opinion about pistol hunters: at close range a .44 Magnum does a good job on a black bear.

Logic and experiments tell me that at close range a crossbow—I shoot a 150-pound Barnett Wildcat—will do a good job on a black bear also. At first I could not be consistent with the 14-inch bolts that came with the bow—made of fiberglass and fletched with vanes. Someone suggested that I try aluminum 2117s cut 16-inches and fletched with feathers. These worked fine. Then I had a problem with broadhead flight—which I cured in the same way I cure broadhead-flight problems I have with certain compounds. I started using the Razorbak-5—a broadhead only 7/8" wide. Broadhead flight became perfect.

From that point on, my difficulties have involved booking a hunt with an outfitter who would tolerate my crossbow.

I can close my eyes and go black bear hunting.

A late afternoon early in June: I'm off the ground fifteen feet high in a tree-blind. I'm dressed in camo—the same camo I wear turkey hunting in Vermont late in May. I wear a headnet and gloves. My shirt sleeves and trouser cuffs are taped tightly around my wrists and ankles to keep out insects. The insects are awful: blackflies, deerflies, and mooseflies are aggressive while the sun shines and mosquitoes hover and buzz when the sky darkens. It is impossible to hear the slight sounds of an approaching bear. The outfitter does not allow insect repellent because of the scent. I have used a 100% DEET preparation anyway—which, of course, will be the outfitter's excuse if I don't see a bear.

With crossbow equipment—as with archery gear—I will have to wait until my bear is quartered away, at under twenty yards, and then shoot to get both lungs. I expect the bear to run, but to fall and be dead at a distance between fifteen and seventy-five yards.

My accuracy with the Barnett was similar to my accuracy with a cam bow: at twenty yards with bolts and arrows I had gotten tight groups into a rotten cantaloupe. However, I have missed big game at twenty yards with a scoped 7 mm rifle, a pump twelve gauge shotgun, a 50 caliber muzzleloader—not to mention the game I've missed with traditional bows and arrows. There is no hunter born not fated to miss sometimes. Even though the Emperor Maximilian of Austria killed 600 chamois with crossbow equipment—proof that the crossbow is an effective hunting weapon—there must have been a few chamois that escaped.

A bear can be wounded with a crossbow as easily as it can with another weapon. But because most bear hunting occurs in the afternoon and evening hours, most trailing of wounded bear is at night. Guides and hunters eager for thrills like to trail wounded bear at night.

Anyway, my eyes still shut, I see my bear fifty yards downwind in a bowl-like depression between two jack pines. He is sitting on his haunches, his huge head rolling on his shoulders, his nose pointing straight up. It seems to me I see many bears in that exact same position: the bear is scenting the bait. He looks wet. But bears frequently look wet. This bear has just arrived from some business in a swamp. I think to myself—now isn't that so damn typical!

I will have to wait and take him when he's much closer.

I will have to wait until next year. Or the year after that. Whenever.

PART 2

NORTHEASTERN MOOSE

CHAPTER 13

*Trapping moose by means of pitfalls, stampeding moose
over cliffs, exhausting moose in crust — snow,
were useful practices to gain meat and hides employed by our
European and Indian predecessors.*

IT IS hard work building a pitfall. But moose in precolonial
America and prehistoric Europe were predictable, and in
places where experience had shown that they would pass,
pits were dug perhaps nine feet deep, nine feet long, and
about four to five feet wide, and covered with branches and
brush. But hunting any large animal was (and still is) a
constant preoccupation and since our predecessors always
hunted large animals cooperatively, undoubtedly the dig-
ging wasn't an ordeal for just one person alone. Ancient
peoples hunted large animals as would a pack of wolves.
They would select one animal from a group or herd, and
somehow isolate it, and then run it down in relays until it
was exhausted and they could kill it. Or get it to run into the
pitfall or to plunge off a cliff. Suitable cliffs are hard to find,
now that I think about it, in the Northeast Wilderness, but
some must have been located and utilized by the Indians for
purposes of felling moose. Writing in 1671, Nicholas Denys
(THE DESCRIPTION AND NATURAL HISTORY OF
THE COASTS OF NORTH AMERICA) doesn't mention

pitfalls and cliffs as Indian moose hunting techniques. This is an oversight. However, he does deal with various other methods, and crust-snow hunting. His book is not in front of me presently, so let us skip over to Scandinavia and the winter hunting there in prehistoric times.

Never conceived of at all in America (where snowshoes were preferred and perfected) skis have been traced back to Neolithic times in Europe—about 11,000 years ago. With skis, hunting on crust-snow was profitable in open terrain, where snowshoes would not have been efficient, in the case of moose weighing 500 to 1000 pounds. An old Finnish epic poem describes ski-hunting thusly:

> "Surely nowhere in the wide world,
>   Beneath the blue sky can there be
> Anything in the lonely forest,
>   Any kind of four-footed beast,
> That a hunter wearing these skis
> Can fail to overtake with ease."

Hunters used spears, bows and arrows, and sometimes nothing but a knife or an axe to kill the exhausted quarry.

In prehistoric times, the moose was widely distributed in Europe. After the last ice age, as deciduous trees forced the pine forests northward when the climate changed, the moose moved northward, remaining only in the enormous tract of wild country across central Europe—which the writers of antiquity called the Hercynian Forest.

Writing in 50 B.C., Julius Caesar (COMMENTARIES) described the many remarkable animals that frequented the Hercynian Forest. "The elk," he wrote, meaning the animal we call the moose, "has no antlers and is entirely lacking in joints in its legs, for which reason it is unable to lie down to sleep. Instead, it is obliged to lean against a suitable tree trunk when it wants to rest. The wily Germanic hunters take advantage of this fact by cutting through the roots of suitable sleeping trees without allowing them to fall. When an elk later on leans against one of these trees, both the tree and the animal crash to the ground and the hunter has only to go up to the helpless quarry and kill it." There was another animal that was not only stiff-legged but also had to walk backwards when eating because of its upper lip which drooped considerably.

Caesar, and other ancient writers, were not reliable observers of the natural world. Medieval writers were often not first-hand viewers, either—several maintained that the moose stored water in a large skin bag under its chin. The water got hot when the animal was chased and it defended itself by squirting the steaming liquid on hunters and hounds—"which then holler and bark most terribly and are covered with burns."

However, writers concerned with natural history and hunting themes were becoming more realistic by the mid-1700s, stressing how extremely difficult it is to kill moose with firearms because of the strong and tough hide; and warning hunters against the quick legs of the moose, which can easily kick and kill pursuers that get too close.

Moose hide was recognized as being strong and tough enough to replace steel armour in many instances. During the 1500s a short mooseskin jacket became a common item of military equipment. Many thousands of moosehides were shipped annually from Scandinavia in the sixteenth and seventeenth centuries to supply the armies of Europe with this fashion in uniforms. The moose populations of central

Europe disappeared. In Sweden, where moose had previously been considered as almost vermin because of its destructive habits in farming country, King Gustav became concerned that the animal might soon die out. By 1538 the moose was on the list of the king's protected animals and moose hunting became the pleasure and profit of royal officials and the nobility. There is much to suggest that the moose and any kind of big game would not have survived in Sweden—and in Europe—without this special kind of protection. A peasant who killed a moose ran the risk of a death sentence or of being banished for life to the wilds of America—and indeed two such poachers are on record as having suffered this fate of deportation.

In any case, by the mid-1700s the moose was scarce in Sweden. Linnaeus, the great Swedish botonist and originator of taxonomic classification, even though he did quite a bit of travelling and observing in the provinces of Scandinavia, never saw a wild moose. After 1789 in Sweden, the moose almost became extinct. Gustavus III signed a decree which permitted commoners owning taxed land the right to hunt any and all game on their properties. "Hordes of people," according to the present-day Swedish naturalist of note, Gunnar Brusewitz, skied day and night, especially in the spring on crust-snow, and moose populations were cut down to insignificant levels. In 1825 a total ban on moose hunting was imposed. In 1836 the ban was lifted but moose hunting was restricted to August, September, October, and November. Late in the 1800s, when bears and wolves had become totally extinct in the south of Sweden and extremely rare in the north, moose populations became viable again in southern provinces and had begun to spread into the northern provinces of Sweden. On the continent of Europe, albeit rather far north, the moose had survived. Moose survival in America, and especially in the Northeast Wilderness, should not be considered quite so miraculous.

Modern Swedish moose hunting methods are unique and interesting and I will deal with them in a later chapter.

500 years ago in the Northeast Wilderness, before firearms and supplies of powder and lead were available, the Indians of what was to be New Brunswick—as well as, probably, the Indians of areas we speak of now as northern New England, eastern Quebec, Nova Scotia, and New-foundland—hunted moose using many of the same techniques of securing meat and hides as prehistoric Europeans. Pitfalls, cliffs, and crust-snow hunting. As mentioned previously, Nicholas Denys (pronounced Denees) doesn't mention pitfalls and cliffs in his discussions. His detailed, fascinating accounts, written in French, were translated into English and republished in 1908. The book is hard to come by and I know of only two copies handy to me. One is at the Maine State Library in Augusta—but as I'm writing this, now, that facility is closed due to asbestos contamination. The other is at the University of Maine Library in Orono and they won't allow me to look at it. I have managed to secure a copy of the original work in French, however. My son's high school French teacher owns a copy in paperback and loaned it to me.

Denys was in the fishing and timber trading business and later a governor of part of Acadia. He was a remarkable observer of nature and Indian ways. He explicitly states that his descriptions of Indian life refer to the years 1600 to 1640, well before "le debasement culturel" of their race.

According to Denys, the weapons that Indians used to hunt moose were bows and arrows and spears. "Their bows

. . . were of maple, an unsplit piece. In fashioning them, they made use of their axes and knives. For polishing them, they used shells of oysters or other shells, with which they poished as can be done with glass. Their arrows were of cedar, which splits straight. They were nearly one yard in length. They feathered them with eagles' quills. In place of iron they tipped them with bone . . . . Their lances were of beech, at the end of which they fixed a large pointed bone."

Denys makes no mention that the Micmac Indians he observed used anything like the atlatl to launch their spears. However, the adoption of the bow and arrow, long since extant, had made the atlatl an obsolete device—as the atlatl had rendered pitfalls and cliffs almost unnecessary. We can presume, also, that the quality of the average Micmac Indian bow was similar to the Sudbury bow—the one made from hickory, circa 1660, on exhibit at the Peabody Museum in Boston—which had a pull-weight of 45 pounds at 28 inches and could shoot a hunting arrow (up in the air at a 45-degree angle) with a flint head 175 yards. The bone heads of the Micmac arrows were undoubtedly lighter and had more range but could not have penetrated big game as well.

In any case, let us get on with how the Indians of the Northeast Wilderness hunted moose—according to Denys, who is our best source for this information. "The hunting of the moose in summer took place by surprising them," Denys wrote. "The Indians knew approximately the places where they could be found. In those localities they beat the woods, going from one part to another to find their tracks. Having found one they followed it, and they knew by the track, and even from the dung, whether it was male or female, and whether it was young or old. By its track they knew also whether they were near the beast. Then they considered whether there was any thicket or meadow near by where the beast would likely be, judging from the direction it was taking. They were rarely mistaken. They made a circle around the place where it was, in order to get below the wind so as not to be discovered by the moose. They approached it very softly, fearful of making noise enough to reveal themselves to it. Having discovered it, if they were not near enough they approached closer until within arrow-shot, which is from forty-five to fifty paces. Then they launched their blow against the beast, which rarely fell to a single arrow. Then it was necessary to follow its track. Sometimes the beast would stop, hearing no more noise. Knowing this from its pace, they went slowly and tried to approach it yet again, and gave it still another arrow-shot. If this did not make it drop, they had again to follow it, even to evening, when they camped near the beast, and in the morning went again to take up the track. The animal being sluggish in rising because of the blood it had lost, they gave it a third shot, and made it drop, thus accomplishing the killing. They then broke off some branches to mark the place, in order to send their wives to find it.

"When the females enter on the rutting-time the hunting was done at night upon the rivers in a canoe. Counterfeiting the cry of the female, the Indians with a dish of bark would take up some water, and let it fall into the water from a height. The noise brought the male, who thought it was a female making water. For this object they let themselves go softly along the stream. If they were ascending, they paddled very softly, and from time to time they made water fall, counterfeiting always the female. They went all along the border of the river, and if there was any male in the woods who heard the sound of this water, he came there. Those who were in the canoe would hear him coming, because of the noise the beast made in the woods, and they kept on constantly imitating the cry of the female, which made him come close up to them. They were all ready to draw upon him, and never missed him. The darkest night was best for this hunting, and also the most calm.

"In the winter the moose does not find good going, because he sinks into the snow, which fatigues him greatly in travelling. To find the moose, the Indians run about from one place to another, seeking wood that was bitten. For at this time of year the moose eat only the twigs of wood of the year's growth. Where the Indians find the wood eaten, they met straightway with the animals, which were not far distant, and approached them easily, they being unable to travel swiftly. They then speared them with the lance, which is the large shaft of which I have spoken. At its end is fixed that large pointed bone which pierces like a sword. But if there were several moose in the band, they made them flee. At that season the moose arranged themselves one after another, and made a large circle of seven miles or ten, and sometimes of more, and beat down the snow so well by virtue of moving around, that they no longer sink into it. The one in front becoming weary, dropped to the rear. But the Indians, who were more clever than they, placed themselves in ambush, and waited for them to pass, and there they speared them. There was always one person chasing them; at each circuit always one of the moose fell; the survivors scattered into the woods, some in one direction and some in another. There fell always five or six, and not a single one could escape. But in those times the Indians killed only their provision, and they only went hunting in proportion as they had need of meat. The hunting of moose on the snow was a main reliance of the Indians in winter, and in winters when the snow was scant, and they could not thus capture the moose, they were often reduced to misery.

"In the winter the hunting of moose was also done with dogs. The dogs of the Indians are a kind of mastiff, but more lightly built. They have the head of a fox, but do not yelp, having only a howl which is not of great sound. As for their teeth, these are longer and sharper than those of mastiffs. There is no hunter who has not from seven to eight of them. They cherish them greatly. If they have little ones which the mother cannot nourish, the women suckle them; when they are large they are given soup. When they are in condition to be serviceable, they are given nothing but the offal of the beasts which are killed. If eight days pass without any animals being killed, they are just so long without eating. Their wealth was in proportion to their dogs, and as a testimony to a friend of the esteem in which they held him, they give him that dog to eat which they valued the most as a mark of friendship. They say that is very good eating. The French that eat it when they are present at their feasts tell great stories that they like it better than mutton. This opinion, nevertheless, has never given me any desire to eat it.

"When the Indians took their dogs to hunt the moose, the dogs would run about for some time, some in one direction and some in another. The one which first met some track followed it without giving tongue. If he overtook the beast, he got in front of it, jumping for the nose. Then he howled. The moose amused himself, and wished to kick the dog in front. All the other dogs which heard it came running up and attacked it from all sides. It defended itself with its feet in front; the dogs tried to seize its nose or ears. In the meantime the Indian arrives, and tries without being seen to approach within shot below the wind. For if the animal perceives him or his smell, the moose takes to flight and scorns the dogs, unless the hunter gives it an arrowshot. Being injured, it has difficulty in saving itself from the dogs, which follow it incessantly, as does also the Indian, who overtakes it and shoots again. But sometimes the dogs, which have seized the ears or the muzzle, drag it to earth before the Indian has come up. They are not inclined to abandon it, for very often they have had nothing to eat for seven to eight days. The Indian arrives, completes the kill, splits open the belly, and gives all the entrails to his dogs, which have a great junket. It is this which makes the dogs keen in the chase."

CHAPTER 14

"The hard part of moose hunting is to find the moose," recalled
Manly Hardy in 1901, referring back to experiences forty years
earlier. "I cannot see any reason why the sportsman should have
any more credit than if he had shot a cow."

I HAVE dug up considerable historical material on black bear
by Manly Hardy, a hunter-writer who had numerous adventures outdoors in Maine in the 1800s. My spade un-
earthed, to turn a phrase, moose literature as well. Hardy's
journals and other writing present a clear picture of what
was happening to the moose populations in the Northeast
Wilderness late in the nineteenth century: just like in the
eighteenth century, professional hunters continued to supply goods to a gluttonous hide industry in America and
Europe. While Hardy, and others like him, were slaughter-
ing the moose here, the moose populations in Europe
(meaning Norway, Sweden, Finland, and western Russia)
were on the verge of extinction precisely because of the hide
industry and also because of habitat changes.

In any case, whatever had happened did not diminish
the adventure of it one bit, and I'm sure readers will appreciate the following gory account written by Hardy about one
particular moose hunt . . .

"We had gone perhaps five or six miles, and were going lengthwise of a valley by the side of a ridge of hardwood, when our dogs suddenly threw up their noses and started off at right angles, going across the ridge and down the other side. It proved afterwards that with the air perfectly calm these dogs had smelled a moose which was on the other side of the ridge more than a quarter of a mile away.

"We soon came to the end of the ridge where another valley joined the one we were following, and we could hear the dogs barking up this valley. As all parties had agreed not to kill another moose for the spring, Philbrook and I wished to keep on our way, but Farrar and Billings wanted to go up and see the moose. They promised not to kill him, but wished to see how large a one the dogs had got.

"Philbrook and I sat down on a pack one of them had been carrying and waited. After a while we heard two pistol shots. We waited a long time, and as the barking still continued, we were a good deal puzzled, as, if the moose were dead, the dogs would stop barking, and, if he were not dead, why did they not fire again. Getting tired of waiting, we went up to see what the trouble was. We found an immense bull, one of the largest I ever saw, standing close by the side of a large spruce. Quite a space around him was trodden solidly. On coming up I raised my rifle, when Farrar asked what I was going to do.

" 'Shoot the moose,' said I.

" 'You wouldn't shoot a dead moose, would you?' asked he.

"On my replying that he did not look very dead, Farrar replied that he had two bullets right in the life nearly half an hour before.

"Farrar then proposed that if I would cover him with my rifle, he would creep up behind the spruce near which the moose stood and knock him down with his ax. Farrar missed his blow, and the moose plunged almost on top of him. I placed a bullet behind his ear, when quick as a cat, he wheeled after me. Billings, on the other side, shot behind the other ear, and he left me and turned on Billings.

"We then retreated to a respectful distance to reload, as the moose would go no further than the snow was trodden.

"These maneuvers were repeated four times in the course of which he received from me four bullets behind the ear in a space not bigger than one's thumb, two from Billings behind the ear and one in the neck. After each charge he would return to his old standing place behind the spruce, where he would grunt and slap his lip at us, throwing the blood which ran from the wounds behind his ears down upon his bell all over the snow. But he showed no sign of being troubled by our shooting.

"Finally I was detailed to go in front of him and shoot him in the curl of the hair. This was a difficult performance, as the snow was well trodden in front of him and he was sure to plunge at me when the rifle cracked. Beside this, he kept his head continually moving, and one had to hit the size of a dime for the shot to prove fatal. I approached as near as I dared and fired twice, each time having to sprint to get out of the way, as I was within about twenty feet. At last Farrar crept up behind the tree and succeeded in knocking him down. It was then found that one of my bullets struck exactly on a level with the curl of the hair about one inch from it, the other about an inch above the first. Into one of the bullet holes I could, and did, put my little finger its length; and the other merely broke through the skull, and I took it out welded together with pieces of bone. This moose had received eleven bullets in all—two directly back of the shoulder, one through the neck, four behind one ear, two behind the other and two in the forehead. The bullets were small, being about sixty of round ball to the pound, but mine were fired with heavy charges of powder.

"In this battle with the moose I do not think that anyone engaged was in the least excited; in fact, had anyone been, firing as we were obliged to and running about on snowshoes as we did, we should have been in great danger, both from the moose and each other. The snow was four feet deep or more, and all in the vicinity of the moose had been wallowed and plowed into pit-holes two or three feet deep with sharp, hard ridges between, making the footing very uncertain. Yet not a man stumbled or tripped in the whole fight. All that was said was in low tones, and no one showed the least excitement either during or after the encounter. In fact, if all had not been perfectly cool, we should have been in more danger from each other's bullets than from the moose, although we all knew that if anyone fell his chances of coming out alive were small. The dogs, it may be said, took no part in the fight; one, which was gun-shy, not coming back till after the moose was skinned.

"This moose was not at all startled when found by the dogs, and made no attempt to escape. He had trodden a yard of at least half an acre, so that it was very dangerous for the dogs to approach him in front, and he seemed willing to fight the whole world. Commonly there is no danger in shooting moose in the snow, as, whether hunted with or without dogs, they almost invariably try to escape, and as soon as they are out of the yard, if they can be overtaken at all, they can be shot at short range without risk. While a savage old bull like this might be shot with safety from a distance, to knock one down with a hatchet is a different proposition.

"This moose showed unusual tenacity of life, but out of a number of instances I will give one which I have known of similar fighting endurance. A.P. Willard and Henry Clapp, of Brownville, while running a sable line under the side of Big Spencer Mountain, close to Moosehead, came upon an old bull which showed fight. Having with them a double-barreled smoothbore they fired all the bullets they had, some five or six, which ran twelve to the pound, at short range. As they used a muzzleloader it was some time before the last was fired. They had with them several changes of shot and also an iron tobacco box, and when their bullets were gone they built a fire, poured the shot in the tobacco box and holding the cover in a split stick melted it down. Then they made a notch in a hardwood tree which they had felled for the purpose, and ran the lead into a long mass; this they cut in two and pounded into slugs fit to be fired. Both these they fired into the moose, going close to him. After a while, as the moose lay down, Willard lashed his sheath knife to a pole with his handkerchief and, creeping up at the back of the moose, crouched and tried to spear him, steadying the pole over a cradle-knoll. The knife struck a rib and broke, and the moose sprang up so quickly as almost to come on to Willard. As each had a hatchet, they next tried to kill him by felling trees upon him, but when a tree was about to fall he would avoid it by stepping out of range. Finally they had him entirely fenced in. Then they tried to kill him by throwing their hatchets. One axe struck his nose, cutting it half off, but the battle ended by his getting possession of both axes and having apparently as much life and fight in him as when they began. As they had no other weapons and it was near night, they withdrew to the camp. On going out next morning with a fresh supply of ammunition, they found him dead. As both these men knew where to hit a moose and could place bullets just as they chose, they were so near, any one of these shots, under ordinary circumstances, ought to have killed the moose in a few minutes; but I believe that an enraged moose will bear a half dozen to a dozen wounds, any one of which would have killed him immediately if he had been still-hunted.

"We had intended to get through to camp before dinner and had nothing cooked with us. As it was near noon when we had finished skinning the moose, we concluded to dine where we were. So we built a fire on skids to prevent it sinking into the snow, making it close by the flayed carcass of the moose. We placed our snowshoes between the moose and the fire, in order to have something to stand on, and, hauling the skin up over the moose, had seats equal to a spring sofa. Each one cut a piece of meat to suit himself, and roasted it on a stick, and each one also roasted one of the marrow bones. The eight marrow bones of a moose, as I know by actual experiment, will yield three pints of marrow, which, when salted, is fully equal to butter. It used to be said that old John Benwit, of the Penobscot tribe, could eat the contents of all eight marrow bones at a sitting. If so he must have had a stronger stomach than all four of us, as we found it difficult to finish one apiece. But we made a good meal, although we had not even salt to go with the meat, and had nothing to drink.

"I had had all the moose-killing I cared for, and though it is over forty years I have never tried to kill a moose since.

While I believe it is fully as honorable for a man who needs money to kill a moose for the hide as it is for one who does not need money to go into the woods and kill one only for the head and horns, still I think it is mean business for any man to waste the carcass of so large an animal merely to say that he has killed a moose. I have always made it a point of honor never to kill anything merely for the sake of killing, and would never kill a deer when I should be able to use but a single quarter, even though I was in need of meat."

CHAPTER 15

According to Peterson, the ancestry of the genus Alces is uncertain. "A study of the available living forms suggests that Asia was probably the center of dispersal."

RANDOLPH L. Peterson, author of the authoritative NORTH AMERICAN MOOSE, speculates that *alces americana,* the moose of the Northeast Wilderness, is probably derived genetically from *alces alces pfizenmayeri,* the Siberian Elk—as would be all the other races of moose. The Siberian Elk, typically found in Northern Siberia, is a relatively large and dark form, similiar to the Alaskan race, but with the nasal processes of the premaxillary bone extending further up the rim of the nasal aperture. Its nose has a more pronounced hump, in other words.

Seven races of moose have been identified. The geographical distribution of them all is circumpolar in the northern coniferous forests of both the Old and the New World. *Alces alces alces,* the European Elk, typically found in Sweden, is a relatively small animal with a broad nasal process of the premaxillary bone extending well up the rim of the nasal aperture. The skull is relatively short. The pelage—the hairy coat—averages more grayish brown in color than North American races and usually lacks the blackish tints found in all other moose races.

Alces alces cameloides, the Manchurian Elk, supposedly found in southeastern Siberia and northern Manchuria, is presumably a relatively small animal. Peterson states that he believes there are one or more antlers of this animal in the Paris Museum, but he isn't certain. *Alces alces gigas,* the Alaskan Moose, typically found in Alaska, is the largest living form of moose with a massive skull, a high occiput, and a wide palate. The taxidermied head and antlers of this one would probably be an inconvenience if you had it up for show in the living room of your mobile home. *Alces alces shirasi,* the Yellowstone Moose, typically found in Wyoming, is of medium-size, with a relatively wide nasal aperture, and a paler pelage than the other North American moose. *Alces alces andersoni,* the Northwestern Moose, typically found in Manitoba, is also of medium-size and differs from the other North American races chiefly in cranial details. *Alces alces americana,* the Eastern Moose, the moose of the Northeast Wilderness, our moose, ranges from Maine and Nova Scotia westward through Quebec to central-northern Ontario, where it apparently intergrades with the Northwestern Moose. Our moose was introduced into Newfoundland. Our moose is of medium-size, with a relatively dark pelage, and with a narrow palate relative to length of toothrow.

If you were to place specimens of these seven races together in a line-up, there would be no doubt in your mind that they were all moose—albeit that their heads and noses had differences, their body-sizes varied, and their pelages were a medley of grayish brown to almost black.

In general, though, the moose is distinguished by his large saddle-horse size, heavy body, long legs, short tail and neck—and by his uniquely high shoulder region, broad overhanging muzzle, and a peculiar dewlap or "bell," a pendulous part, not exactly but almost comparable to the wattle of a bird or a fold of skin hanging from the throat of an aged person. The nose is covered with short hair except for a bare spot between the nostrils. Adult males develop large antlers with broad palmate blades. The hoofs are long, narrow, and pointed. The front hoofs are larger than the rear ones.

In spring the upper pelage varies from grayish brown to almost black. The lower pelage is lighter. The pelage gradually fades through the seasons becoming almost gray by winter.

Peterson points out the distinct possibility that wapiti, caribou, and moose may have an extinct relative represented by the stag-moose (*Cervalces*) of the Pleistocene epoch, which is about a million years ancient, more or less. He quotes William B. Scott (A HISTORY OF LAND MAMMALS IN THE WESTERN HEMISPHERE): "The only known *Cervalces* skeleton, now in the Princeton Museum, is in Pleistocene deposits. The skeleton is very much like that of the moose; the bones of the neck, trunk and limbs are almost identical in the two genera, but skull and antlers are very different. The nasal bones are much less shortened than in the moose, an indication that the proboscis-like muzzle was less inflated. The antlers are unique, though in a general way like those of *Alces,* they are much less palmated and they have, in addition, a great trumpet-like plate of bone on the lower side of each antler; this plate is not known in any other member of the *Cervidae. Cervalces* has not been found in the Old World, yet it must have originated there from the same stock as the moose and accompanied the latter in its migration to North America." Fossils of wapiti, caribou, moose, and stag-moose have been taken from the deeply frozen deposits that overlie the gold-bearing gravels of Alaska. These deposits, dug into by prospectors eager for the yellow metal, are quite ancient and so is the moose, evidently.

For the purposes of this book, however, I can only presume that readers are more interested in the modern moose—specifically *Alces alces americana*. So let us get on with some description of moose life history, and try to start somewhere at the beginning.

A healthy cow in good habitat produces, most often, two calves each year. I have myself observed a cow with three calves in Maine. Mostly I have observed cows with twins, however. Some cows fail to breed through no fault of their own, apparently. In many areas bears (and in former times, at least, wolves and mountain lions, too) kill and eat calves. In other areas, if the habitat is not especially bountiful, a sort of natural birth control takes place—a cow though bred will produce but one calf or none at all. In this instance the biological principle to keep in mind, according to Peterson, is as follows: "Preservation of a species is dependent on the interaction of its biotic potential and environmental resistance."

The life cycle of a moose begins with its conception during the breeding season. This occurs early in September to late in November with the peak period being the last few days of September and first few days of October. Cows are receptive for 7–12 days but conception can only occur during one day of that time. The interval between heats is 20–22 days. Most of the conceptions occur during the prime time of late September and early October, however. Female moose can breed as yearlings and thereafter yearly until 18 years of age. Most seem to skip a year now and then. Figures as to the number of barren cows (or cows apparently not accompanied by calves) in a moose population vary greatly, but it seems to be from 10 to 60 percent. In many areas the lesser bulls defer to the dominant individual who obviously can service just so many cows and no more. When the big fellow gets past his prime or dies somehow or gets harvested by a hunter, more bulls breed more of the cows. Anyway, the rate of reproduction of *Alces alces americana* is low. The rate at which *Alces alces alces* reproduces is much higher and probably is the fruit of decades of hunting pressure, which is mostly directed at calves and bulls in Sweden, in spite of the great efforts by the authorities to control this preference. (Calves are very fine to eat. Bulls have horns which are attractive as decorations. Cows too frequently are tough to eat. Hunter-partiality is easy to understand.)

The gestation period for moose is about eight months, with most of the calving occurring in late May and June. If a cow has young with her from the previous year, she will aggressively drive them away so that she can concentrate all her attentions on the newly born. A just-born calf weighs 25–35 pounds and usually can't stand at all the first day. A calf is not mobile very much at all its first week of life and is virtually defenseless. It is protected, however, by the fierce supervision of its mother.

A just-born calf is light reddish brown in color with a dark dorsal stripe. It has short hair and lacks the spotting found on young whitetails. The "bell" is clearly evident. According to Peterson, a calf when only a few days old has a high-pitched cry which is almost human in quality. Of course, a moose calf when young is fed mostly with milk. It has been calculated that a wild cow moose can produce about 40 gallons of milk during a lactation period. A domesticated cow moose has been observed to produce 113 gallons over a similiar time period. These were measurements made in a Russian wildlife park and the moose involved were *Alces alces alces*. A calf will begin chewing on plants when it is only a few days old. By two weeks of age it is foraging regularly. A calf grows rapidly its first five months. Actually it is believed that no other wild animal in America grows so rapidly as the moose. By October of its first year a good one should weigh at least 250 pounds dressed and should make the best possible meat for the table. Believe me, I've had my freezer filled with old bulls and hardly more acceptable cows. Took my wife and I and my son two years to eat that last old cow and I have since sworn never to harvest anything but a tender, fat, little calf. It is really easy to understand why moose calves are so popular with hungry bears.

While the only hazards to life and limb for the moose in Sweden are hunters, trains, cars, radioactivity from Russia, acid rain from Germany, and a higher-than-needed reproduction rate, the moose in the Northeast Wilderness have a mortality problem because of whitetail deer, wherever the two are in close association. Whitetails are the normal primary host of a parasite that causes a neurological disease in moose. Deer suffer no apparent harm from this agent. Moose die from it, however, as it invades the brain and causes incoordination, lameness, stiffness, weakness, circling associated with blindness, and eventually paralysis. The parasite has caused declines in moose populations in Nova Scotia, New Brunswick, and Maine.

Generally, however, even a moose that is quite healthy and not suffering from "moose disease" is apt to give the impression, upon the occasion of an accidental meeting in the woods, when you're picking berries or mushrooms, of emotional instability. George Shiras, after whom *Alces alces shirasi* is named, wrote in 1912: "No antlered animal of the earth is more obtuse and stolid than the moose, and no animal, when finally alarmed, is a greater victim of an increasing and progressive fear than his. At times it seems almost impossible to alarm them, and then when this is accomplished, one wonders whether they ever recover from the shock."

"The ears often serve to alert the animal," according to Peterson, "the eyes to investigate, while the final stimulus, causing immediate reaction, is transmitted by smell. When approaching an animal upwind silently in a canoe we were usually successful in getting within close range. Even when the animal detected our presence, rarely did it rush away without stopping and turning to look at us for a second or third time. When travelling noisily upwind through the bush we were occasionally surprised by a moose a few yards ahead watching our every move. Frequently if we stopped and stood silent the moose would continue to watch us, perhaps move a few steps and turn to look again before finally moving away."

The rutting bull does not behave that way. If he meets you casually—that is, by accident—he may imagine or wish that you are another bull challenging him. His heavy antlers dip from side to side as he moves in stiff, long strides in circles around you. His antlers hit and shred trees and shrubs and he browses with hasty, jerky movements and exaggerated intensity. His eyes are fixed on you. What you have to do in this situation is either shoot the bull, climb a tree and start yelling at the bull, or run as fast as you can to the road and get in your truck. It may not be hunting season.

You may not have a gun. There may not be a tree. You could be scared speechless when you're up the tree anyway. Maybe you can't find your keys or you can't get the engine of your truck started.

In any case, there is a fair to good chance that the bull is just bluffing and that he won't hurt you at all—especially when he notes that your scent is not that of another bull moose.

CHAPTER 16

It is interesting to note, but not surprising,
that there has been a shift in moose density and distribution
from the early 1940s to the present in Maine and elsewhere in
the Northeast Wilderness: the forest management practice of
clearcutting has created habitats that moose prefer.

FOOD and climate are the most important aspects of habitat
for moose. Large quantities of forage must be produced to
maintain moose. The quality of the forage is also important.
A moose needs proteins, fats, carbohydrates, minerals and
vitamins. Every moose habitat is not the same and so the
food habits of moose have to vary considerably. For the most
part, however, the needs of all moose are met by the con-
sumption of early successional woody browse—young
trees in the early stages of regrowth following the distur-
bances of fire or logging. *Alces alces shirasi* makes do with
mostly willows for its nutritional needs. Firs, aspens, and
birches satisfy *Alces alces americana*. Moose everywhere are
adaptable. As Peterson points out, moose are able to use
their long legs to good advantage in travelling the length
and breadth of their boggy, brushy, slash-filled habitat. In
these same areas other animals find travel impossible.
Though Peterson seems to be skeptical that this is really the
case—clearcutting of vast areas is unattractive and the im-

mediate impulse one has is to disapprove of it—clearcutting actually creates moose habitat that is almost exclusively moose habitat. Only insignificant populations of predators and whitetail deer and caribou can share this kind of environment so the moose is pretty safe from fang and claw and disease as well.

There is considerable seasonal variation in the types of food moose eat and in their methods of feeding. The moose has to be browsing in the winter, naturally—biting off terminal twigs and 1/2-inch thick branches of coniferous and deciduous trees. In the early spring, as the sap is rising, moose chew maple bark and whatever else is newly green. When fresh leaves form from buds on limbs, a moose strips the leaves by pulling the limbs through his mouth. One investigator observed that when a moose feeds in summer undisturbed he moves slowly, "taking a few mouthfuls from one place and some from another with an average rate of movement of three yards every five minutes." In the warmer months, a fair portion of *Alces alces americana*'s diet consists of aquatic and semi-aquatic plants. In fact, the casual and scientific observer will frequently discover our moose in the middle of some shallow lake during the day in the summer. One good reason for this is to get a respite from bothersome insects—the ones that attack during the day—but the most significant reason is the food. Moose are most active feeding around nightfall and daybreak, then they chew their cud or sleep, but since moose are powerful swimmers and enjoy the water, there's no reason at all why they shouldn't be getting wet in the local lake when the sun is high. Reports Peterson: "Water is definitely one of the preferred elements in the habitat of moose. When feeding on submerged aquatic vegetation they occasionally dive for plants in water over 18 feet deep. They were frequently seen to submerge so completely that not a ripple remained in the water near where they went down. In the majority of cases the rump would float to the top and break water before the animal raised its head. Occasionally animals were seen to make at least a 180-degree turn while completely submerged, and at other times they would seem to roll to one side while attempting to stay under. The actual length of submergence was slightly under 30 seconds. The greatest time actually checked was 50 seconds, although some appeared to remain under slightly longer."

Moose may be overtaken when they are swimming by two people vigorously paddling a canoe or by a boat with an outboard motor. Biologists find this predicament of the moose convenient when they need to attach radio collars to the animals for scientific reasons—to determine the size of an individual moose's range and seasonal changes in habitat preference and looking at pond-use activities by moose. Also, in the Northeast Wilderness, it is not easy to count moose from an airplane, to get an estimate of the moose population, because the subjects are hidden under trees. If moose using particular ponds could be counted, and cow/calf ratios studied from year to year as an index to reproduction, then the direction (i.e., either up or down) of a census could be calculated. Biologists doing field studies must weigh, measure, sample, and count—and devise means by which they can accomplish these duties. Francis Dunn, a Maine biologist, developed a water-capture technique on moose that makes current field studies fruitful. According to Dunn, in a 1970 issue of *Maine Fish & Wildlife Magazine,* to radio-collar a moose ". . . requires that the moose be maneuvered into deep water where it cannot touch bottom and is forced to swim. This is accomplished by two men in a small boat. Once the animal is swimming, his headway is controlled by keeping him directed toward deep water. The man in the bow places a lasso over the head of the cow or the antlers of the bull with the aid of a long pole. The lasso is equipped with a stop so the rope cannot be pulled tightly around the moose's neck. The rope then passes through a pulley arrangement in the bow, and the boat is pulled up next to the moose. The bow man reaches out, places the collar around the animal's neck, and snaps it in place. Once the motor is started and the approach begins, only a few minutes elapse before the collar is intact and the moose is released. Once alongside, the moose loses most of his fight and usually tries to escape by putting his head under water. On one occasion, a young bull was lassoed while he still had a mouthful of aquatics. From the time of capture until the transmitter was placed, he made several attempts to escape by ducking his head beneath the surface of the water. When released, he swam away still holding the mouthful of food; upon reaching shore, he calmly munched the plants while keeping a wary eye on the men in the boat."

In Maine, prior to 1966, only limited efforts were made to estimate moose population levels. Before that moose densities were calculated by guesswork; and I imagine the following conversation could have taken place: "What's the moose like in your area, George?" "Pretty thin, Fred." "How about your area, Mike?" "Well, when George and I were in his vehicle doing creel-counts, first week of June this year when we had all that rain, we almost hit a cow with a calf when it was dusk. Ha, ha, ha! I'd say they're getting thick over by the beaver bogs around Blackfly Lake where the paper company has just put in that new logging road."

"Better show me on the map, Mike."

The 1966 aerial census covered all of Maine and 6,831 moose were counted. Many more might have been counted if they hadn't been hidden by trees. The limitations of aerial-type moose-surveys were recognized immediately. Deer you can count pretty well from the air because they winter in congregations in yards. Moose are solitary. A herd of moose may simply be a family grouping of five animals—one cow plus two calves and two yearlings. A bull moose in the winter from the air may not be recognized for what he is. Instead he looks like a big, gray, granite rock. More imaginative field methods were called for from which moose population figures could be extrapolated as a supplement to aerial surveys. And Dunn did it.

The capture system he devised is used in Maine presently by biologists studying moose. In recent years the equipment has included a 12-foot aluminum V-hull boat, a 6 h.p. motor, some half-inch nylon rope, and a 12-foot set pole. The moose-study area in Maine is north where logging interests are quite active. Numerous shallow ponds full of aquatic vegetation dot the area. This is habitat considered ideal for *Alces alces americana* — or at least the best that can be offered in Maine.

Radio collars are placed on moose in order to study movements, habitat use, and natural mortality. A 1983 issue of *Maine Fish & Wildlife Magazine* explained the moose-telemetry technique this way: "The antenna is swung in an ever-decreasing arc until the point at which the signal is the loudest is reached. A compass bearing is taken at that point, as well as from a second such point on a different part of the study area. These two bearings are plotted on a map, their intersection representing the location of the moose.

"The home range of each moose is then determined by measuring the area of a figure formed by connecting the outermost radio locations. The average summer home range of the six cows [referring to a particular small-scale moose-study over a time period of two summers and one winter in which six cows were located 543 times] was 10 to 13 square miles. The home range during the winter of 1981–1982 averaged 0.5 to 1.0 square miles. The deep snow of that winter obviously restricted the movement of the moose to a small area. Mild winters such as 1982–83 permit moose to move around more; it allows them a larger home range.

"Range telemetry showed us that cows also use a small home range—less than one square mile—during late May and early June. This corresponds to the calving period. Having been bred in September during the peak of the rut, most cows will give birth in late May, about 240 to 246 days after breeding. They typically pick secluded, well-vegetated sites in which to give birth. The limited mobility of the calf during the first few days of life prompts the cow to remain in a small area. By mid-June, the cow and calf are once again on the move and using the full extent of their range.

"Habitat use is determined by plotting each moose location on a cover-type map. The cover type, as well as the distance from water, is recorded for each location. These are then tallied by type to determine which habitats are being used. A habitat type is typically considered preferred if it is used proportionally more than what is available. For example, if a moose was relocated in hardwood stands 30 percent of the time, yet hardwoods only made up 15 percent of the habitat in the area, we would consider hardwood areas preferred habitat. However, if moose were found in hardwoods only two percent of the time, we would consider moose to be avoiding hardwoods.

"In this study, sources of water (lakes, ponds, beaver flows, brooks) and open bogs were preferred habitat during the summer. Young and second-growth stands of softwood were also preferred. Moose seemed to avoid mature soft-wood and hardwood stands, as well as mature and second-growth hardwood-dominated softwood. Mature stands provide little in the way of browse for moose. Their favorite summer foods are more easily reached in the young and second-growth stands.

"The observation data provided some interesting insights into pond use behavior. Moose came to the ponds primarily to feed on the aquatic vegetation. Terrestrial browse still makes up 70 to 90 percent of the summer diet of moose, however. More than 800 moose were seen during 1,120 hours of observation. Date, time of arrival and departure, length of stay, sex, and weather condition were recorded for each observation.

"Moose in general tended to use the ponds in the early morning (5 to 8 a.m.) and late evening (5 to 9 p.m.). July proved to be the best month to see moose; August was the worst. The most interesting observation was that cows with calves dominated the scene in early September. This observation was totally unexpected. No other researchers of the North American moose have reported such an observation, yet I saw it two years in a row. This finding should shed new light on the state's aerial cow-calf surveys and may help to increase the precision of the ratio estimates."

I am not trying to write about moose in a truly scholarly or scientific manner. But I am definitely obliged in this work to deal with historical and technical information—and bits of personal correspondence, as well. Two examples follow:

★★★

"As we toured that area, I chanced to spot a cow moose not far off the road. I dismounted my bike to begin a careful stalk, a hunting technique at which I am considered expert. Perhaps I was too quiet, because I came right upon two calf moose hiding in the undergrowth. Just as I stepped on the babies—where their hip joints join their rib cages—their mother saw me. Probably she heard me first, as I gasped at the feel of flesh through my bicycle shoes, and turning she saw me. No matter, because I immediately headed back for the road taking a more direct route than during the stalk and checking for trees to climb or to hide behind while making the dash. The cow moose was charging and quickly closing the gap between us. Finally I found a decent, tall-enough fir and managed to scramble up some six or seven feet. The cow arrived—ears laid back, snorting and sniffing only inches from my bicycle shoes.

The PSE wheel bow, the one set at 65 pounds that I mentioned earlier, might have been a match for this moose if I could have placed an arrow between her ribs. Several fir branches were in the way and would have prevented drawing this bow. When the cow moose left, satisfied that I had been rendered harmless—perhaps she smelled something— I returned slowly to my bicycle and changed into my other polypropylene undershorts.

★★★

One morning we had visitors near the encampment— two biologists. Not seeing our Cannondale bicycles and unaware of our presence (the L.L. Bean tent is camouflaged with plastic leaves and grasses) the two men were in the weeds at the edge of the pond mushing mosquitos and enduring midge molestations. I gathered from their conversation—which I could clearly understand—that moose research was their object here. The light was of a pre-dawn dimness with mist rising from the water and leaping fish making rings. "Yellow perch, piscus jaundice vulgarus," the biologist with the long, white beard said. He looked like Moses. "The yellow perch is very catchable, grows to small sizes generally, appears not to be very smart and demonstrates no dash or style. There are numerous hungry fishermen around, however, and that's why yellow perch rate high on so many hit lists. They are catchable all year round—unlike trout and salmon. They are not fickle–a wide variety of lures and baits attracts them."

"What are you babbling about?" the other biologist asked. He wore thick glasses and chewed tobacco. He spat. He was alert for moose-splashing sounds, however, and frequently checked the pond-shore opposite with binoculars. Moses handed him a squeeze-bottle of insect-repellent lotion. Spitter glanced at the little orange container, his expression bemused. "That will make these state-owned binoculars sticky," he said, handing the bottle back.

"In North America," Moses continued, "there are ninety-nine species of perch—and only one is called a perch, and that's the yellow perch. The largest member of the perch family is the walleye—a gamefish of note often nearly 20 pounds in weight. The most ubiquitous is the yellow perch —everywhere but these regions rated as the best eating of all the panfish and actually preferred in many areas over trout."

"Shut up," Spitter said.

But Moses was nervous and obviously not the old-soldier biologist with big-game experience that Spitter was. Viewing them from my peep in the tent, I imagined that Spitter had probably thrown capture-nets over black bears many times and dragged them out of winter-dens on numerous occasions, and to him an alces alces americana was no great difficulty, especially dealing with it from the relative comforts of a boat while it is helpless in the water. I actually heard them discuss that. Helpless? Moses was not so sure. A menace? Moses indicated that he wouldn't want to be swimming close to a moose that was swimming. At least not in the same swimming pool. His eyes hazed over, and he started his prattling lecture again—evidently he was more or less of a fisheries biologist impressed into temporary service with this moose project. "Near-shore in large lakes, yellow perch average 6–8 inches in length," Moses said, observing dispassionately a sudden swirling six feet away and the dorsal fin of a pickerel briefly displaying. "In deeper waters," he resumed without significant pause, "they can get up to two pounds in weight. Actual sizes anywhere are determined by natural predators and by fishermen. In warm, weedy water where pickerel and bass abound, yellow perch grow bigger than they do in lakes like this one, where the only serious predators are stocked salmonids. Whereas trout and salmon are hesitant in chomping down on fishes with stiff, sharp dorsal spines, pickerel and bass are not that particular. In any case, in waters with few natural predators, yellow perch numbers become too great for the food supply, and average perch length is less than 6–8 inches. That is the case in many ponds and small lakes, including this lake."

Suddenly Spitter grunted. He had spotted a moose, a cow. He touched the fishery-man's elbow, making sure he was alert finally. The two biologists waited until the moose was in the pond and swimming. The object was to cut the animal off from shallow water and the shore and to keep it swimming in deep water. Tensely now, they waited. At last, when the moose was in position and occupied with feeding, the two slipped silently to the boat. Moses, when the moose's head was under water, started the engine and the boat plunged from the shore. Quickly then he idled the engine and cut it, and the boat glided slowly to the target. The wind favored Spitter and his assistant, and the moose was munching unconcerned. With the distance a mere six feet, Spitter flashed out with the long pole and slipped the noose around the moose's neck.

The noose in place, Moses in the stern pulled the rope tight. He got his beard caught between the rope and the boat and screamed. Spitter leaned over, and as he made reassuring conversation to the startled beast, he placed a one-pound transmitter on a pink collar around its neck, got a good fit, then buckled the transmitter down.

The noose was still in place, but the moose strained in panic now. Moses still screamed. An insect-cloud almost engulfed the scene. Spitter quickly clamped ear tags on the animal, then released it from the rope. Then he spat—a long, arching display of juice that plopped perfectly, glup, in the water. Moses, finally quiet, started the engine and used the boat to herd the moose back to shallow water. The moose heaved onto the shore and then trotted into the brush and pines a short distance before stopping to shake itself. It looked back at the boat briefly and then with long-legged strides quickly disappeared.

CHAPTER 17

Usually it takes months of planning to arrange a moose hunt in the Northeast Wilderness. You have to be lucky and win a lottery in Maine. You have to win a lottery and also be a resident in New Brunswick. In Nova Scotia you have to be a resident. Other regulations apply in NS, too. In Newfoundland and Ontario . . . I think you had better call them up on the telephone. But in Quebec, how can I get there again? A quelle heure commence le moose hunt?

THE booking agent I was talking to over the telephone was slightly disagreeable, I thought, and for that reason I trusted him. If he had been entirely pleasant, you might think he was selling you no fish, no game, a tent, a latrine, and poor food at an expensive price.

"Moose," I said. "Where can two people go?"

"Ah, Jolliffe . . . the moose, he is the ghost of the woods."

"Are they all dead?"

"No, no, no. He is very popular, though, and everyone wants to shoot him. But Jolliffe, if I may call you that, Mr. Norman, we have 500,000 caribou, so many caribou . . ."

"Next year caribou," I said. "This year moose."

The booking agent sighed heavily. I could hear him flipping through papers on his desk. He cleared his throat.

"Ah, the long, plaintive call of a cow moose that issues from your birch bark canoe," he said, "it is perfect as it vibrates through the evening mist lingering over the small mountaintop lake. Eagerly you wait, listening intently for a reply as the minutes go by, one by one. You know there's a moose somewhere—you've seen his fresh tracks along the well-beaten game trail that winds down off the hillside now ablaze with autumn color. There's the pungent odor of falling leaves in the air and, now that the sun is three-quarters hidden by the horizon, a certain chill has come over the land."

"Any sign? Droppings? Tracks?"

"Yes, yes, yes. As you settle deeper in the warmth of your old hunting coat your eye catches a movement off to the left and there, against a backdrop of dark spruce, he stands: the ghost of the woods, Mr. Norman. As you stare in disbelief he grunts a throaty answer to your call."

"Are there lots of moose in Quebec?"

"*Certainly,* Jolliffe!" The response was emphatic. "Biologists estimate that Quebec's moose population numbers between 100,000 and 150,000 head, a number that's difficult to determine accurately because of their rapid spread into new territories. The ghost of the woods will test your skill as a hunter. It is a trophy to be proud of. The beautifully palmated antlers may spread as much as five feet on the eastern moose, truly a hunter's trophy. The recommended firearms are scope-mounted rifles with at least 2,000 foot-pounds of energy at 100 yards. Scopes should be sighted in for 100 yards."

"We will be bowhunters," I said.

The booking agent sighed heavily again. "You will be hunting after the archery season," he said. "I can not schedule you before the second week of the firearms season. Also only one moose per two hunters."

"That's okay," I said.

"Rudimentary accommodations or full-service?" he asked.

"We want first-class," I said.

"Next year, Mr. Norman, please remember one hunter may take two caribou."

"I'll remember."

Reservations were made for us at Richer Lodge the second week of October, 1985. There has been a cardboard box of scrap—literally, that's what it is, scrap—sitting by my desk for a year now relative to the above Quebec experience. It contains black and white negatives and prints, color slides, two broken arrows, notes, tape-recordings, correspondence, and cash receipts. The two broken arrows—Camo-Hunter XX75 2216s with broadheads intact—were fired into a moose. I handled the broken shafts yesterday and an ink-black, liquid substance poured from one onto my jockey shorts. The notes are entitled THOUGHTS WHILE SITTING IN A MOOSE BLIND and I am perplexed to see that they are incomplete. I recall scribbling a virtual novel. Only once were conditions inappropriate to take writing implement in hand: when I was cold, it was raining, and the pen after a time refused to make an impression on the paper. Then, as I recall, I curled up in a fetal position in one corner of the blind and tried to go to sleep, hoping, of course, that a moose would not blunder along, because Pierre, our guide, was watching my position from 100 yards away with his binoculars. The tape-recordings are extensive and intact, however, and there are six of them. Excerpts from the first three would be pertinent to this narrative.

In any case, let us examine certain items of the scrap more carefully.

ITEM: *An envelope marked "Quebec moose," containing receipts*

This envelope I wish I had discovered before I did my income tax last January. It contains my Permis De Chasse 3538508; seven assorted cash-register receipts from department stores in Bangor, Maine, which add up to $70.34—for socks, recording tape, batteries, a nail-clipper, gloves, glue, and dental floss; a Visa receipt for slide film and processing envelopes, $84.97—no mention of black and white film, which I also took with me. I probably bought that earlier and then lost the receipt. Barnett shopped at these department stores and spent about the same as I did—let's say $155. Also, David spent $450 of Barnett International money on London-Boston-Bangor air-fare.

As I recall, the actual expense of our full-service moose hunt in Quebec may be fairly stated as $2167. We could have cut some corners, of course. It is obvious, though, that the cost is going to be in the $1000 per-person category for anyone duplicating our experience.

ITEM: *A letter from the booking agent, dated Sept. 17, 1985*

"In reference to the numerous telephone conversations we had, it is a pleasure for me to confirm the dates of your moose hunt (bow hunting); October 5th to 11th, 1985.

"The outfitter Raymond Richer from 'Richer Lodge', located on the Echouani Lake (north of Mont Laurier City, east of La Verendrye reserve) is very happy to greet you and will do everything possible so that your stay and hunt are a success. As discussed with Mr. Raymond Richer, the rate for an American Plan is $408 per person for the stay. The cost for the guide during the stay is $400. You may phone please (819) 449-1613 for directions to 'Richer Lodge'. You may write my friend Raymond Richer at 110 Cavanaugh, Maniwaki, Quebec J9E 2P8. I have enclosed the brochure 'Fishing, Hunting & Trapping, 1984–1986' in which you will find all the necessary information on the hunting laws in Quebec. Please accept, Sir, my kindest regards."

ITEM: *A letter from a person who had hunted moose out of Richer Lodge, dated Sept. 17, 1985*

"[The booking agent] asked me to write you. I thoroughly enjoyed my moose hunt at Richer Lodge. Although I was unsuccessful at bagging a moose, I never had a doubt that I was situated in excellent moose country where an opportunity for a shot could have come at any time. That I didn't shoot a moose was simply hunter's luck. The camp was both efficient and comfortable. It was one of the best I've ever visited. And the food was superb! If [the booking agent] asks me again to write prospective customers my recommendations, I will feel happy to do so. I'm looking forward to coming back to Richer Lodge this spring for the bear hunting and to sample the excellent walleye and pike fishing. Those walleyes and pike I saw caught there while I was on the moose hunt almost made me want to put down the rifle and pick up a rod! Raymond helped to make my hunt such a pleasure. Sincerely."

CHAPTER 18

I have survived several adventures with moose,
some amusing, some dangerous, and some just grunting work.
I prefer the amusing kind.

As readers may have surmised by now, often my hunting is done with archery equipment from an elevated position—a tree, or a knoll with a blind, or a step-ladder in a clear-cut. I inhabited a moose blind for two evenings in Quebec on a knoll. Before my Quebec experience I had several moose-contacts. A moose approached my step-ladder once, walking down a deer trail, pausing to munch at poplars. I sat on the ladder, which I had camouflaged and tucked inside a clump of poplars. My outline was not conspicuous and I could see over much of the clear-cut. I knew what would happen before it happened, of course. I was suddenly eyeball to nose with a startled bull moose, who took several good sniffs of the deer-lures on my boots—Tink's doe-in-heat urine on one and Tink's red fox urine on the other—before he charged off gracefully through the slash and raspberry bushes. As I think I have pointed out, moose have poor eyesight—just good enough, I imagine, to avoid large trees. Small obstructions are of no consequence. Moose have fine noses, however, and sufficient intellects not to be fooled by a peculiar mix of odors elevated ten feet among poplars.

After all, why should a female deer in estrus and a urinating red fox be together up a tree? A moose is bound to ask himself that question.

Another time when I was up a tree—probably asleep—I suddenly heard a branch snap behind me and I instantly saw a moose burst forth. One calf was with her some distance in the rear. Both were on the path I had used earlier to my tree-blind. The hair along the cow's spine bristled. Her head was low as she stomped up the path, snorting. I guessed this moose was agitated.

Before hunting that afternoon I had applied a quantity of fisher scent—very pungent—to my boots and pants. The fisher is a furbearer related to the ferocious wolverine. Though smaller than the wolverine, the fisher seems to threaten the safety of young moose. At least that was my conclusion based on what I was observing just then. Obviously the fisher scent had effectively covered my scent.

The cow bumped my tree with her hip and stomped around it several times. Finally, after ten minutes, satisfied that the self-befouled fisher was not about to descend to do battle, she departed with her calf.

In the spring, a cow protecting her calves can be especially threatening. In the fall, a rutting bull is frequently spoiling for a fight. If he's only bluffing about it he tends to be pretty convincing. Any moose any season of the year is dangerous if he's a road-walker. I was driving my pickup on a gravel road one spring night in eastern Maine, going about thirty-five with my high-beams on, when an enormous shadow leaped from an embankment—all flailing hoofs and bouncing antlers. The head of the apparition smashed through my windshield, his ears tickling my nose. My passenger—Clarence Greenleaf—is covered with shattered glass. I'm pinned to my seat by the moose.

"Cut his throat or shoot him," I tell Clarence.

"Isn't he dead already?"

"He's breathing hard," I say.

"His antler is damaged."

"Get your gun and shoot him," I say.

But before Clarence can collect his wits, the moose removes his head from my lap and staggers away into the blackness and the pine trees. Clarence is picking bits of glass out of his beard, starting with his mustache first.

"I saw him before he jumped you," Clarence says. "I tried to reach the steering wheel."

The game warden said I could have the animal if we found it. If we found it quickly much of it would be excellent for my freezer, he said. If we found it very much later than that he indicated that the bears and coyotes would probably appreciate it more than I would.

I wasn't especially thrilled. I had several hundred dollars worth of damage to my pickup. As it turned out we never found this moose in any usable condition—two weeks later on the same gravel road at approximately the same spot as the accident, during daylight in the afternoon, I observed a moose with a limp and a damaged antler.

The majority of hunters who take part in Maine's one week moose season—previously late in September but in recent years the third week of October—do so for the opportunity to obtain meat. Questionnaire results compiled by the Fish & Wildlife Department reveal that 58% hunt for meat, 40% for sport, and 2% for other reasons. Also revealed: moose hunters averaged 22 hours of hunting time, although some individuals hunted less than 30 minutes, and others hunted for 80 hours; and moose hunters sighted an average of 3.8 moose while hunting.

The first day of the first modern Maine moose season— in 1980—was one that interested the press very much. As many press people participated, getting stories, as there were moose hunters in the woods getting moose. Most of the journalists clustered around the tagging stations, especially the one in Greenville by Moosehead Lake. Press with TV cameras were filling their machines with dead-moose footage. Press with tape-recorders, notebooks, and Nikons were interviewing anybody they could grab, including each other. A dozen people representing *Outdoor Life* and the other major blood-sport magazines were smoking their Dunhill pipes and wearing official looks of Grave Concern. *Sports Illustrated* (I think it was) had a crew making a movie of the crowding and shoving, comparing the event to the excitement prior to a major athletic contest. All of the magazines were taking turns riding in the Fish & Wildlife airplane over the moose-hunting zone around Greenville hoping to observe hunters actually shooting moose.

I spent the day—at least the early morning part of it —riding in a pickup truck with two hunters and their guide.

"Where's the best spot on the moose to shoot him?" I asked the guide. Four of us were jammed into the front seat of the pickup. The guide—hired, of course, to provide a moose for this occasion—was driving.

The guide laughed, fogging up the windshield. "I would say right on the butt of his ear. He drops right in his tracks and you don't have to go looking for him . . . . Lift your legs so I can shift."

"Might not be good for taxidermy that way," I said, lifting.

"Oh, I forgot. This is going to be a legal moose. But still I'd shoot the butt of his ear. He won't drop fast enough if you shoot his lungs."

"People who poach moose shoot the butt of his ear?"

"Oh, yes."

"What kind of rifle do they use?"

"Anything. Even a 22."

"A 30–30 then would be good."

"Oh, definitely. In that particular spot it would be good."

"What are the chances that your clients here will have success?" I elbowed the client next to me because, after all, the question was a jocularity. But the two hunters, wedged against each other and the door, remained silent and inscrutable. As a journalist, I do not profit much by silence and inscrutableness. On the other hand, a flood of information I can't manage either; and the opposite of inscrutableness—a frothing-at-the-mouth kind of thing—is frightening and perhaps dangerous to be near.

"Their chances of seeing a moose are damn good," the guide said. "Whether they can hit one or not is beyond me. I've never seen them shoot."

"It's raining," I said.

The guide turned on the wipers. "This won't last," he said.

"Do moose poachers call moose? Or do they happen onto them close to the road and then follow them a short distance into the woods?"

"We don't call. Oh, no."

"Do the people around Greenville favor a moose season?"

"Oh, no. Not around here. Moose are a tourist attraction. We want lots of them—tourists and moose."

"This rain is not going to be good for photography. Did you hear a weather report?"

We listened to the radio, driving along on hard roads that progressively became more narrow, and then on gravel roads with bumps and depressions. Obviously the hunters had a destination in mind. When we arrived at the rim of a yarding area, the guide turned off the truck lights and then his engine and we rolled to a rest next to a pile of rotten pulp logs. The rain had stopped and a portion of the rising sun was brightening the scene, reflecting gray clouds and blue sky in scattered pools of water. The desolation was colorful—yellow whips of poplar surrounded the yard. Dripping, foot-high spruce grew in the yard, oddly placed. One section of the yard was devoted to several lines of red pine, no higher than the spruce, but these had been planted by the paper company according to a scheme. We rolled the truck windows down all the way and sat listening.

"Okay, you boys had better get out now," the guide whispered, after about two minutes. He extracted binoculars from behind the seat.

The hunters opened the door and slipped from the seat and removed their rifles from cases in the back of the truck. They left the door open and I eased over to be more comfortable. The damp air had an earthy, moldy scent. The hunters slammed clips into their rifles—autoloading carbines in 30–06 caliber—and disappeared out of sight beyond the pile of rotten logs. In a moment we heard shooting. The first rifle, five shots. The second rifle, two shots and a shout: "It jammed!"

The guide and I climbed from the truck quickly and peeped over the piled logs. More shouts: "Can you see him?" "He's running!" "Fall, you bastard!" "Is he going down?" "Yes, he's down!"

The guide peered through his binoculars and then handed them to me. He pointed while I focused. Finally I could see the moose—a nice bull, repeatedly attempting to regain his feet, and failing. His tongue hung limp from one side of his maw. "Doesn't look like they've killed him decently," I said.

"I bet there's only one bullet in that moose," the guide said, shaking his head. "They shouldn't be shouting."

"Liver?"

"Maybe kidney."

We were whispering. The hunters returned and ducked behind the logs with us and they were whispering now also. The hunter whose gun had jammed confessed that he had been using reloads. The other hunter said that he had bought his ammunition yesterday at a grocery store in Greenville. All of us criticized the hunter with the reloads because it is common knowledge that reloads are not reliable in auto-loading rifles.

"I was holding on his heart when I had the misfire. I ejected, then I had another misfire. I couldn't believe it."

"Oh, we thought your rifle jammed."

"That's what I thought at first. The bastard should have been down twenty feet from the road. He's a good size moose!"

"He has a good rack!"

"Quiet! We don't want that son-of-a-whore up, I'll tell you, because he might go an awesome mile."

"Awsome?"

"Too long."

"Very long."

"Then you got to drag him out that far. Let's give him twenty minutes to bleed out and die."

The reintroduction of a season to hunt moose in Maine is not the result of conservation practices—although sportsmen give themselves some credit and Fish & Wildlife officials are managing the developing situation rather well. The new moose season in Maine is basically the result these past decades of colder winters with more snow, larger timber harvesting operations, and a declining deer population—but we've discussed all these things in a previous chapter. Also, of course, moose are appreciated more than in former times in part because of an effort by the Maine Publicity Bureau to convince vacationers that moose symbolize Maine as much as the Eiffel Tower symbolizes France and the iceberg symbolizes Greenland. The moose is, in fact, the official Maine animal—as the chickadee is the state bird and the pine-tree cone and tassel the state flower. However, the chickadee is too diminutive to photograph well and the pine tree glory is somewhat uninteresting.

So Maine sportsmen were not exactly eager to hunt moose and they deserve some credit for the population explosion. Maine game wardens deserve some credit, also. The fine for illegal possession of moose parts can be $500, plus three days in jail, and confiscation of rifle, chainsaw and other implements—i.e., airplane, boat, truck.

In September, 1980, at about the time of Maine's first modern season, two provinces in northern Sweden, Norrbotten and Vasterbotten, were also having a moose harvest. The conservative Swedish newspaper, *Svenska Dagbladet,* reported the event as follows (and I translate loosely): "It's a bang, bang world for 60,000 moose in Norrbotten and Vasterbotten. 20,000 have to be culled. The hunters in those provinces have more than double quotas this year. The herd has to be limited because of traffic safety.

The moose are too many and hunters are doing their best to shoot all they see. 'It is going to be difficult to kill 90 moose,' says Aldegard Larsson, one of 13 hunters assigned to area 33. 'Years ago when we started hunting there weren't that many moose. You had to be happy with six animals to share. I suppose it's our own sensitivity that has made the herd increase. None of us will shoot calves. Most of us won't shoot cows. So there's no wonder the herd has increased.' "

Vasterbotten and Norrbotten cover an area almost three times the size of Maine—89,000 square miles vs 33,000 square miles. The 1980 moose population in Maine was estimated at 30,000. That was a conservative figure. The 1986 moose population, as I am writing now, is much higher, of course. Obviously moose density in Maine is similar to densities in Vasterbotten and Norrbotten—and the population of the somewhat smaller Swedish *alces* is considered a risk to human life and property—i.e., a traffic-safety problem. The European moose has a reproduction rate higher than the race of *alces* in Maine. Multiple births are more frequent in the *alces* population of Sweden. Moose in Maine have a reproduction rate of 23–27%. For moose in Sweden, I do not have a reproduction-rate figure. A good guess would be about 30%.

CHAPTER 19

Dressing a moose and getting him out of the woods requires a plan and a list. It may not be necessary to follow the plan exactly or necessary to use every item of equipment on the list.

I HAVE accompanied other moose hunters in Maine—most notably two seventeen-year-olds. Anita, my wife, is friendly with a mother of one of the boys, and she so harrassed me that I agreed to provide protection for the endangered and his friend the duration of their proposed adventure. Anyway, I figured I could get a magazine article out of the experience. Neither youth had ever taken big game before, although both confessed to letting lead fly on several occasions at deer. No cigars, however—no blood, no hair, no nothing. Their discussions in my presence centered around this rifle versus that rifle, cars, and girls. I calculated, therefore, they were more interested in ambience than in blood.

The afternoon of the fourth day of the 1982 moose week, I heard shots from where I told the boys to take a walk, then whooping and hollering. Then joyous shouting. Remember, now, their experience wasn't of the sort encountered by the hunters I was with in Chapter 18. Those fellows got their moose after about thirty minutes. These boys here shot an *alces* after spending considerably more time at it.

I remember hoping they had killed a calf.

"Twenty points on him!"

"I saw fresh tracks going this way. So I stood on this log and I could hear twigs breaking. I thought there could be something big down there. 'Donny,' I said, 'there's something big near us.' Then we heard grunting sounds and more twigs snapping. Then we saw the cow and the bull. The bull was going crazy—grunting and trotting around the bushes. By accident moving we started making noise. I would walk, Donny covering. Then Donny would walk and I would cover him. The bull saw us and started walking toward us. But he got behind a tree and started smashing it. I made some sounds at him, so he quit the tree . . ."

"I had the crosshairs right between his eyes 75 yards away but I didn't dare shoot . . . I was shaking like a leaf."

"Donny shoots him and he starts to run and I shoot him. Then I move closer and shoot him again and he drops."

"He was already on his knees."

"Congratulations, boys. Now the work begins."

It is real work, too. A 200-pound whitetail or a 500-pound black bear is a lot less work than a 1000-pound moose. Obviously. And servicing five deer or two bears is also less work.

Any moose hunting adventure requires equipment other than the normal hunting and camping gear. Here follows a list of those extra necessities:

> 1 chainsaw
> 1 large sheet of polyethylene
> 2 sharp hunting knives
> 1 sharpening stone
> 2 rolls of paper towels

50 feet of nylon rope
1 axe
1 bone saw
2 large plastic bags
10 game bags
1 pound of black pepper
2 come-alongs
2 pack boards
2 Coleman lanterns

The heart, liver, kidneys, and tongue should be saved —into the plastic bags for convenient and clean transportation out of the woods. You might also want to save the muzzle and the testicles. All of these parts have to be cooled quickly. Remove them from the plastic bags, wipe them down good, and put them on ice in a cooler or refrigerator.

Now, speaking personally, of course, I am not much interested in the above organs as edibles. The heart I might go for, however, because it's only an internal muscle. But I've never had deer heart, bear heart, caribou heart, beef heart, pork heart, lamb heart, or the heart of any bird. I have been invited to share in a big-game heart now and then, but the hunters preparing it for the table were doing so more for the religious rites involved and not because they were hungry. The heart of any beast really does have significance, but I'm not going to eat it.

The liver. As I recall, Pierre-the-guide on my Quebec adventure requested the liver of the moose that had been killed. We gave it to him eagerly. If the language barrier had not intervened, I would have tried to explain to Pierre what I knew about moose liver, which actually pertains to all livers. The liver is a detoxification organ. It is a gland that secretes bile and acts to form blood and to metabolize carbo-hydrates, fats, proteins, minerals, and vitamins. Unfortu-nately it is unable not to concentrate within itself certain heavy-metal pollutants. Lead and mercury immediately come to mind, but there are others. These heavy metals arrive on the moose's dinner table, so to speak, with the rain. Acid rain is the result of atmospheric smoke, caused mostly by industrial activity, that arrives with the wind from areas outside the Northeast Wilderness, killing all life in certain susceptible lakes, and depositing a thin layer of heavy-metal dust everywhere. Too much of the dust ends up in the livers of moose, not enough to harm moose espe-cially—except maybe they get headaches now and then. If peole eat these livers the heavy metals end up in their livers. If they eat deer livers or bear livers and even beef and chicken livers—if these animals were raised in the north-east—the heavy metals end up in their livers. I never eat the wild or domestic livers of anything raised anywhere. These days you can never be sure of what an animal eats along with its regular food.

I can't imagine why anyone would want to eat kidneys, either. Kidneys are excretory organs. They maintain proper water balance and regulate acid-base concentrations, of course, but mostly I associate them with urine production. They taste like urine, too. Nothing can disguise that taste. Years ago, when I was courting Anita, her best friend prepared a meal for me which could only have been a test of my digestive abilities: I was required to partake of kidneys on a skewer. These had been cut in half, with bacon added, then steamed for five minutes, brushed with butter, dusted with cayenne, and then grilled with onions and green pep-pers. I vividly recall the recipe. The friend's family—

mother, father, sisters—all of them regarded me with twisted, sadistic smiles, as I sliced into and bit down upon this *pièce-de-résistance* of their family cuisine. When Anita and I were eventually joined legally in matrimony, only then did I assert my right not to eat kidneys. It was a tricky, delicate business, however.

Moose tongue probably should not be in the organ-meat category. I have always enjoyed beef tongue. I have had moose tongue only once—belonged to a calf, and that tongue had been in a pickling solution for two weeks before Anita boiled it. We ate it with a gravy seasoned with pounded cloves, mushroom-ketchup, and cayenne.

I have never had the opportunity to eat moose testicles. The Quebec moose was a cow and I was again frustrated. In any case, male moose taken in the rut obviously have testicles rich in androgens, and I suppose I wouldn't be adverse to a taste-test. Anita would probably suggest that I eat them raw, but I imagine they probably ought to be pickled like the above calf-tongue for two weeks, skewered, then grilled with onions and green peppers. Mustn't forget the cayenne.

We are getting very close to the subject of moose-muzzle, now. I can see that I can't pass over it unobserved, or delay it until the next chapter, or hope that I will mention it in the epilogue. But I have had no personal experience ever eating the nose of a moose. However, Manly Hardy—whose affairs with moose were reported in Chapter 14—is able to supply excellent information.

"It fell to my lot to cook some moose noses, of which we had a good supply. The moose nose and the beaver's tail are considered the two great delicacies of the woods. As few now know how to prepare them, it may not be amiss to record the way the hunters did it. No amount of scalding will remove the hair from a moose nose, and the Indian method was to singe them on the coals and then to scrape them. But this always gives them a burnt taste, so I have always preferred to skin them. This is most easily done by splitting the nose through the septum and pinning one half firmly down with a fork, so that it will not slip about while working on it. Afterward the nose is boiled several hours til it becomes tender. Beavers' tails are usually roasted on a stick before skinning, or sometimes made into soup with rice."

Regarding moose nose, Hardy doesn't mention anything about a gravy to go with it. I've just asked Anita what she would recommend and naturally she thinks something spiced with pounded cloves and cayenne would be excellent. I have consulted a Swedish cook book I have, but find no recipe for moose nose there—although it does contain numerous other moose recipes. In some desperation I even contacted the Hermit of Blackfly Lake and received back a brief note from that personage: "If you want to find out how to enjoy moose muzzle and other exotic parts, read THE MOOSE FROM FOREST TO TABLE; a book available for $5.50 from the Institut National Des Viandes, 10216 Lajeunesse, Montreal, Quebec H3L 2E6. It's 192 pages—37 of them with recipes." In any case, when I do get a chance to eat moose nose, I think I might prefer it cold, even jellied, and dressed with a Dijon mustard.

Let us return now to the equipment list mentioned above—starting with the chainsaw. The chainsaw is a very tempting tool, but should not be used to cut down the backbone of a moose. It makes a mess, I assure you, even when the chain is lubricated with extra-virgin olive oil. The chainsaw you use only to cut a path out of the woods from where the downed moose is located to the nearest road.

The polyethylene is for dumping the moose guts onto as you are doing the field-dressing. When you've finished with this unpleasant task, then you drag the poly sheet well away from where you're working on the moose. Dressing a smaller animal it's no problem just to leave the guts on the ground and then to move the carcass a safe distance. With a moose it's much easier to move the guts a safe distance.

The list requires two sharp knives, but probably it should specify four of these. Two people are going to be cutting and skinning at once and while this is taking place a third person should be resharpening the two knives they started with. Keep your fingers crossed that this third person knows how to use the sharpening stone. The paper towels are for wiping the knives, your hands, and inside the cavity of the moose after you've gotten everything onto the poly and dragged it away so that the incompetent person sharpening the knives won't be stepping or sitting in the guts or befouling himself or the good parts of the moose.

The rope. The nylon rope is for making the dressing of the moose easier. Although field-dressing of a moose is not much different than doing it to a deer or a bear, the moose can be dressed easier if the legs are pegged out. It's called "pegging out" and the process is as follows: lengths of rope are strung from the legs of the moose to nearby trees or—if there are not sufficient trees convenient—to pegs cut from trees and pounded into the ground with an axe. That's why the axe is on the list. The bone saw is on the list because it might be necessary to saw bone. The plastic bags I have talked about already.

If the moose can't be hauled out of the woods immediately, registered, and placed in a cooler, he should be skinned and quartered immediately. If the weather is frosty and a good tree is handy, he could be elevated with the two come-alongs (on the list) off the ground for a few hours until you can hire a skidder or a horse. But by and large skinning and quartering is the best thing to do. Moose hide is thick and retains body heat more efficiently than deer hide.

The meat—dusted with black pepper—goes in the game bags. The game bags get tied to the pack boards—one bag per board. You make several trips to your pickup. If you are doing all this at night you will need good lights. Flashlights won't help you see nearly as well as Coleman lanterns.

Of course a camera with a flash system should be on the list, too. It will help you recall the miserable situation later so that you can avoid a repetition.

CHAPTER 20

*Even though the Northeast Wilderness is no longer a frontier, a
backwoods kind of humor—the tall tale told with a straight face
being a significant portion—still prevails in the area.
Alces is the central character in one such tall tale.*

NICHOLAS Denys (whose historical material we became familiar with in an earlier chapter) described the Northeast Wilderness as a kind of fertile frontier. "Along both shores of the [Penobscot] the trees are beautiful, and in great abundance, such as oaks, birches, beeches, ashes, maples, and all other kinds that we have in France. There is also a great number of native pines which have not the grain of the wood very coarse, but they are of forty to sixty feet in height without branches, and very suitable for making planks for building both for sea and land use. There are also many firs, of three species and [the one called spruce] has a grain much more compact than the others, and is much better fitted for making masts and is the best . . . . Quantities of bears occur, which subsist upon the acorns that are found there; their flesh is very delicate and white as that of veal. There are also a great many moose. . . .

"From the [Penobscot] as far as the [St. John] there may be forty to forty-five leagues. The first river met with along the coast is that of the [St. Croix]. There are in this river a great number of islands in a cove of great circuit. At the head of this cove discharge little streams in which are found salmon, trout, bass, and along the coast are caught cod and other fish of all kinds. . . .

"Ascending [the St. Croix] two or three leagues, one comes upon little islands covered with firs, birches, some oaks, and other woods. Farther up this river is a fall which hinders vessels from going farther, though canoes can travel there. I have not been able to learn its extent. Some mountains appear there in the upper part, and a number of meadows bordering the place; of these some are rather large. All the woods there seem to be fine; there is a great deal of oak, and of other kinds of trees of which I have already spoken. It is claimed that this place is where the Sieurs de Mont and de Champlain wished to construct a settlement, to such a degree had they found the locality good and pleasing beyond all others they had seen.

"[In the river St. John] in the pitch of the fall is a great hollow, of about three or four hundred feet around; this is made by the rush of the water as it passes between two rocks which form a narrow place in the river, an arrangement rendering it more swift at this spot. In this hollow is a great upright tree which floats, but no matter how the water runs it never gets out; it only makes its appearance from time to time, and sometimes is not seen for eight, ten or fifteen days. All of the Indians who passed by there in former times rendered it homage. They called this tree the Manitou, that is to say the Devil. The homage which they formerly rendered it consisted of one or two beaver skins, or other peltry, which they attached to the top of the tree with an arrow head made of moose bone sharpened with stones. When they passed this spot and their Manitou did not appear, they took it for a bad omen, saying that he was angry with them."

North of these rivers described by Denys is the present-day, modern Nepisiguit of New Brunswick, flowing north and east some 80 miles to empty into the Bay of Chaleur at Bathurst. History knew the Nepisiguit as an outstanding salmon habitat—but this fact has been largely ignored by American flyfishermen because of the superfluous publicity given the major New Brunswick river systems.

I caught two salmon out of the Nepisiguit when I fished it a few days in August, 1986. Clarence shot a roll of film of one exploit, then he slipped on a rock and lost my camera. The outfitter's father kept us amused in the evenings with stories, at no extra charge.

★★★

"When I was working for the company, Mrs. Gray and I used to look after the lodge year round, and once a party comes in for fishing trout. I was told by them boys about one fellow, supposed to be one of the best fishermen around, who bragged that he fished everywhere. He had fished in the old country. He had fished them tuna that weighed seven hundred pounds. There's no use to tell him anything about fishing, they said, because you can't tell him nothing. They told me to make up a story to tell that fellow. Anyway, when this party goes away, the fellow they told me about—and two more—come to the lodge.

"I thought about telling that fellow a story. I thought about it a long time. And one day we start talking and finally he gets going about all the fishing he had done. He had fished everywhere. Anyway, in that big lodge I had one of my own moose heads mounted. It was a big moose head that had a spread of seventy-two inches. That was a record moose head. That night the fellows had a few drinks and they were talking and this fellow starts to look around after he had been so windy about his fishing, and he says, 'Mr. Gray, who shot all them animals that's mounted in this lodge?' I says, 'Lots of the guides. I have a few deer heads here and so forth.' He says, 'My God, that moose up there is an awful great big moose.' I says, 'That belongs to me.' He says, 'In the name of God, how did you ever kill that?'

"I says, 'Oh, I didn't kill that with a gun.' He says, 'Well, how did you kill him?' I says, 'I fished him.' He says, 'You what?' I says, 'I fished him with a line and hook.' He says, 'Don't try and tell me rubbish! I've fished every-wheres, caught them great big tuna, and all them kind of fish. Don't try and tell me rubbish!' So we pass us a little drink around and we look at the moose. He says, 'How could you fish a moose?'

"I says, 'Well, there's a small little camp down by the river where it's maybe fifty yards across to the other side, and every morning I'd go down, all alone, and that moose would be on the other side eating lily pads, where there was a kind of swamp. After he had ate so many lily pads he would look all around and put out his great big pink tongue. So one morning I go down to the camp with my rod because I wanted to catch a few trout to cook for my breakfast. Sure enough that moose is there. I just looked at the distance and I wonders when that moose sticks out his tongue if I'd be good enough to haul that backcast . . . and cast . . . and hook him by the tongue. If I could just be lucky enough, then there was no harm in trying.

" 'So I keep casting. I get out thirty yards, forty yards. It's a good fifty yards across. But soon the hook is falling pretty damn handy, maybe two or three feet from him. I had to watch my backcast because of the alders and I didn't have too much backing on my line. But finally the hook was falling a foot from him. And just the next cast he puts up his head, sticks out his tongue, and I hook him! The tongue is a tender place in a moose.

" 'I start reeling. I had a pretty good line. And he's coming across the river hooked by the tongue and the little camp is right there behind me thirty feet in the woods. The moose is getting pretty handy and I'm getting scared. See, I don't want to bring him out of the water and onto dry land. A big moose will charge if he's on land! So the idea just hits me to back into the cabin, and shut the door on the line. So I did, and there's the moose twenty feet from the cabin hooked by the tongue. I put the rod down, because I couldn't haul or nothing, and go to the kitchen of the camp and start to look around. Somebody who had been there hunting the fall before had left a bottle of turpentine. Well, I know that turpentine burns. So I goes out the back door of the camp, lift the moose's tail . . . I'm very careful . . . and I splash him with the turpentine. You should have seen what happened! There was a flat rock the size of a good rug and that moose sat on it and started to rub himself. He rubs . . . I'm watching all this . . . and he rubs and he wears himself out . . . until just his head is left and I hung his head right there.'

"That fellow never talked to me about fishing again."

CHAPTER 21

In September of 1983, Rick Clowry of Hartland, Maine, participated in a Maine moose hunt. His report—called "Stick & String Bull"—appeared in The Maine Bowhunters Association Newsletter *sometime later. It appears again below.*

THE announcer droned on, reading name after name. Names from all over the state were being drawn from the big barrel to participate in this year's moose hunt. 300, 400, 500, 600 names called. Only 300 left, and I hadn't even heard a name resembling my own! The chances were getting slim. 650 names called. Still nothing. 694. Man, I want a chance with my bow at . . . "Number 695, Rick Clowry, Hartland, Maine!" The ceiling still has dents where my bow tip punched it as I leapt from the floor. Yeah, I was holding my bow for good luck. I think that other hunters share this feeling with their special pieces of equipment, also.

After several minutes of an out-of-body experience, I realized that I hadn't listened which zone I was to hunt in. A few phone calls later I knew that I would be hunting the Central Zone of the five-zone hunting area.

Preparing for any hunt to me is half the pleasure. I'm like a kid at Christmas. And a moose hunt in northern Maine requires careful planning. You have to go prepared to be totally self-sufficient. So, as you might expect, my summer went by in a flurry, and as September rolled around my mind was always on the up-coming hunt.

As in most situations like this, something has to go wrong just to add a little more anxiety to your already hyper-nervous system. This situation was no exception. About eight weeks before the hunt I separated a limb on my Bear Custom Kodiak Takedown Recurve. This, of course, was the bow I had intended to use in the hunt. Talk about a bad omen!

I immediately called Cherokee Archery where I had bought the bow and talked to Ken Ulmer. Ken put in a call to the company and luckily they had a pair of limbs in stock to fit. They were 60" and 60 lbs. at 28" draw. This was great! I had been shooting 50 lbs. and stepping up to 60 lbs. was something I had been wanting to do, especially with the upcoming moose hunt. I'm a firm believer in shooting the heaviest draw-weight that can be shot ACCURATELY for hunting purposes, and I wanted a lot of punch for my moose, should I be able to get a shot. The problem was would the limbs get here in time?

For the next seven weeks I practiced and practiced with my backup bow, a 52" Kodiak Magnum Recurve, 50 lbs. at 28" draw. I was good enough with this bow. I had taken deer with it before, but my confidence lay with my Take-down Recurve. Thanks to Ken, the limbs finally made it. I was left with only five days before the hunt, but I was grateful to have them at all. I wore out a target, frayed a string, and suffered—needless to say—a few sore muscles, but I did feel ready and confident, out to 40 yards, by the time we left, September 17th, for points north.

I drove to Indian Pond Campground and set up camp with my subpermittee and friend, Robbie Robbinson of

Albion, and his friend and business associate, Cliff Perkins from Massachusetts. The weather was terrible but our spirits ran high in anticipation of the hunt. We met some good people who were fishing the ponds and having a good time enjoying the outdoors. They were extremely helpful and told us of a huge bull who had frequented the cove on the pond two mornings in a row, along with a very good cow.

Now things were looking up. Sunday morning they took me out in their canoe to see if he was there—and he was!

It was foggy and he first appeared as a large rock in the pond—then he slowly raised his massive horns, dripping with water. What a beautiful animal, king of his empire, unchallenged by any in the area. His bell dangled in the water and then he violently shook his antlers as if in defiance of our presence. He ran before we could get any closer than 200 yards. This was a wary bull.

I consider myself a pretty confident person with my equipment, but in the presence of such a large and magnificent animal any man, who can be honest with himself, feels somehow inadequate, no matter what the weapon.

There had never been a moose taken legally with a bow and arrow, prior to 1983, in the state of Maine. Many bowhunters in the state were aware of this fact for the first time last year and everybody in bowhunting has been holding their breath, knowing that the first officially bowbagged moose would most surely fall in the near future. There were five bowhunters that I knew of this year who were drawn for a permit and they were all very good hunters. We were all hoping to be the first. I was so excited and up after seeing the bull that I decided to spend the night on the shore and make absolutely positive that if he came back as he had the last three mornings I would be there with my stick and string. Robbie packed me a lunch and I camped out with my sleeping bag.

That night on the shore of the lake was one of the most memorable in my life. About 8:30 with the moon up and a cold hotdog sandwich in my belly, I heard a branch snap and then I heard the steady splash of water as a moose came into the cove from my left—the direction the bull had gone earlier that morning. My heart was like a jackhammer and my mouth was very dry. I saw legs first as the body was still blending with the shoreline shadows. It was moving right out in front of me and as the moon reappeared from behind a cloud I could make out a very good cow, just casually feeding along in the knee-deep water, not more than 25 yards from me. Then I heard another moose coming into the water, suddenly there he was in all his splendor. Antlers glistening in the moonlight, he came up behind the cow and grunted to her. I couldn't believe that I was here undetected on the shore of a remote, northern Maine lake with a trophy bull and cow not 25 yards from me. They fed and mulled around in the lake directly in front of me from 50 yards to as close as 15 yards. You really begin to realize just how large a moose is when a 1200 lb.-plus bull with close to 60" antlers is 15 yards away in the moonlight and you are tucked down behind some tall grass in your stocking feet, with no place to go.

I am human, and it was very tempting to take my moose then, but I wanted to be first and I wanted to be legal, right by the book. The moose and any game-animal deserves to be hunted fairly. I didn't want a cheap victory.

They stayed in front of me till 1:00 a.m. and then the bull moved off to the opposite shore and bellowed. The cow followed him and they left the lake.

I didn't get much sleep between the moose and a drenching thundershower at 4:00 a.m. When dawn finally came I was cold and miserable. No moose showed that first morning, and at 9:00 a.m. I hiked around the lake and walked back to camp. After relating my experience of the night, I changed and slept for a few hours.

I spent that evening and the next morning at the same spot with no sightings. Tuesday evening I paddled the canoe to a spot where I could watch the cove till dark and seeing nothing returned to camp. That night we helped some people in the campsite get a spike bull out from across the lake. It took till 1:00 a.m. to quarter the moose and pack it to shore, paddle it across the lake, and load it in their truck. We were all beat and crashed in my tent. The alarm went off at 5:30 and I literally fell out of bed. My mind wanted to go but my body was refusing. I had been changing my camouflage every day to keep scent down, but this morning I just pulled on my camo coveralls that I was wearing when we packed out the moose the night before. I smelled like a moose. I had hair and blood all over me, but I really didn't care. I was too tired. My partners were sleeping soundly so I didn't bother to wake them.

I grabbed my bow and climbed into my Renegade. Where should I go? For some reason I just felt like riding. The Jeep top was off and the cool morning air helped to wake me up as I drove along the dirt road.

I had an urge to go back to where we had paddled the moose out the night before. To this day I don't know why. It really didn't make any sense with all the noise we made just 4–5 hours before, but I have learned to trust my instincts as much as possible and go with a hunch when hunting, and this luckily proved-out again.

As I approached the lake I killed the engine and coasted up to a stop behind a huge shale pile. The sun was on the lake and it was quiet and beautiful. I sat in the Jeep and scanned the opposite shore with my binoculars. I had been there for about two minutes when I heard the familiar sucking sound of a hoof being pulled from black mud. I brought the binoculars down slowly and peered through the alders. Just then I saw movement. My heart began its familiar pounding as I made out the antler of a bull, on this shore, not 50 yards from me.

I had my 444 Marlin in the Jeep with me and could have shot him right from the Jeep. My mind toyed with the idea. Do I take the easy way? Or do I do what I intended to do in the first place?

I decided that I would rather stalk him with my bow and hope for the best. I eased out of the Jeep and moved in slow motion around the shale pile to my right. I remembered the path leading down to the lake from the night before and it came in very handy in picking my way through the alders. The trail was very steep and loose so it was painfully slow stalking. It was then I realized that the wind was blowing right at the moose. I was trembling and sweat trickled off my forehead and down my nose. I could see him now and he was looking out across the lake, seemingly without a care in the world. I was just 25 yards away but had no shot—the alders were just too thick.

He suddenly jerked up his head and turned to face me. My mind was racing, calculating—he had smelled me, but what he smelled was all that moose on me. Also, I was totally camouflaged and not moving so that maybe confused him. We stared at each other for a solid minute. I noted every detail about him—his bell, antlers with double-palms, whites of his eyes, and the wiry look of the hair on his back. At times like these it's so very hard to know what to do. Should I try a shot? No, too thick! Do I sprint to the edge of the shore and get off a quick shot? It crossed my mind that the moose-scent on me might make him charge. So I waited it out, my bow in front of me, the cat whiskers trembling on the string and my heart trying to blow off the top of my head!

He suddenly again turned broadside and looked up the lake. I knew I had to move. I cat-footed another five yards. The moose turned his head and looked up the lake again and I saw where I wanted to be—another five yards more and I could get off a good shot. Five yards is a long ways when you're stalking an animal and are close to a shot.

I finally made it! I had arrived at my moment of truth. Here is where all my practice and time either payed off or didn't. I had to crouch a little to take advantage of the opening in the alders. With the moose still looking up the lake I began to draw. Slowly back the bow came. I picked a small, dark spot behind his shoulder—a little up from halfway. I was almost to anchor. "Concentrate on the spot," I told myself. "Don't look at him—just the spot." I touched the corner of my mouth and the arrow flashed. Looking back at the moment, it seemed to happen in slow motion. The arrow disappeared in his ribs with a heavy thunk and then splashed into the water in the other side—complete penetration. The moose grunted at the impact and loped about 20–25 yards. He stopped with his feet spread and looked behind him. Then he lowered his head and coughed. A good lung hit. Slowly, like a building falling over, he swayed and caught himself. He then swayed again and made no attempt to stop himself this time. He was dead before he hit water. I watched him for a minute and he never moved. I was shaking and barely kept from shouting as I walked out into the water and retrieved my arrow.

I have killed two deer with my bows and now a moose, and have seen a bow's effectiveness on bear. None of my kills have gone from my sight before dropping. A bow and razor-tipped arrow is a deadly, quiet, clean and humane way to take game.

CHAPTER 22

I once prepared a casual treatise on calling moose.
I queried the blood-sport magazines for a publisher, but none
stepped proudly forward. I have consented to include the
significant portion of that opus here:

THE shadows of the trees got long on the water as the sun
began to sink behind the hills in the south. I didn't have my
compass, but my Indian guide, whose name was Pierre,
tilting his head at the gold orb, said, "That south." Where
the sun rose this morning, Pierre had tilted his head and said,
"That north." I couldn't argue with him because I didn't
have my compass then either. Anyway, as the sun was
sinking, a loon up the lake, east or west, was calling softly,
probably happy because it was getting close to his time to
get to bed, and he was bored with fishing, constantly fishing. Actually, I could never figure loons because they are
never really fishing, as I understand the word. They are
hunting. Fishing is with a line and a hook. Hunting is chasing after something, even if it's a fish. But no matter.

Dusk was about to fall.

Pierre—he told me several times the tribe he belonged
to, but I forgot—dropped his paddle and let the canoe drift.
His paddle was a strange affair fabricated of animal hide and
a stick. Unfortunately he dropped the paddle in the water

and it floated away from us. I thought to myself—we will try to pick it up later in the dark. Meanwhile, however, Pierre lifted something to his lips. The whiskey bottle. I thought to myself—he will be putting the birchbark horn to his lips next. Surely he will. And that's what he did. Pierre blew into the horn.

The call sounded extremely, extremely like a cow. Well, of course, like a cow moose. But what surprised me was it sounded so much like a cow cow. But then I began to think—how can an Indian have a name like Pierre? So I ask, "How can an Indian have a name like Pierre?" Just before he's about to blow into the birchbark horn again.

And that question made him, he said later in another conversation, screw up the call. At least the sound wasn't, he said, exactly perfect. Fortunately when he made this less than perfect call, the loon that was up—or down—the calm lake from us had started to call again himself. The loon was plaintive this time, as if he was sleepy and yawning and with one foot in his nest for the night.

So, as Pierre made the bad call, and the loon made his sleepy call, suddenly I heard a branch break among the poplar trees in front of us. Please understand that all these were sounds occuring at the same moment. Pierre hissed to silence any more questions that I might have at the next moment. He put his ear to the birchbark horn, tensely concentrating. He lifted the whiskey bottle to his lips again. It gurgled. Then he licked his fingers and stuck them in the air to test for any indication of a breeze. No breeze, but there was a slight movement of the air. Obviously the movement was in our favor because Pierre turned to look at me, lifting his brows. He called again with the horn—a properly soft and mellow call this time.

I heard more twigs snapping and the brushing sound of a large animal brushing through the brush. My heart was pounding and the hair on the back of my neck was bristling—a condition that could have been avoided if I'd time to go to my barber before this hunting trip.

When the bull moose stepped out of the poplars I lifted the 280 I had borrowed from a friend, put the crosshairs of the scope on the beast's chest, and yanked the trigger. At the sound of the explosion, the bull whirled around and disappeared. I fired again anyway. "You missed!" Pierre shouted. "Again you missed! Damn!" He smashed the birchbark horn on the gunnel, drained the whiskey bottle and threw it into the lake. Then he asked me, "For christsake, where's the beaver-tail paddle?"

I shrugged and emptied the rifle of the three remaining, unfired cartridges. Then I handed Pierre the rifle and that's how we paddled back to the lodge. We would have made faster progress with the beaver tail but I don't think Pierre minded being leisurely because of the opportunity this gave him to have a good, long conversation with himself. I had to explain to everyone at the lodge—the manager and the staff and the other guests hunting—I had missed an eighty-yard target. Completely missed it, according to Pierre. No need even to check—to look for blood and hair and falling-down signs and that sort of thing.

Moose are the biggest members of the deer family. It is hard to imagine missing one at 80 yards with a decent rifle, except perhaps if the canoe is rocking and the rifle isn't decent. Calling is the most exciting way to hunt moose, whatever object you have in mind: meat for the freezer or rack for over the fireplace. Calling, however, is by no means a surefire guarantee of these things.

When you are calling a moose you can't be certain what he will do—come charging in like a rhino or cat-footing in like the ghost of the woods, suddenly and surprisingly, or be a lazy, good-for-nothing and not respond to calling at all. That kind of moose needs hormone shots . . . those synthetic steroids? Of course, you can't blame a moose for showing some intelligence: he doesn't like the sound of the calling, and you can hear him moving around restlessly, even calling back, but prudently refusing to show himself.

The smartest moose I ever encountered—one that could only have intuitively realized that I, and not another moose, was calling—was an individual that answered my call three evenings in a row from the same spot, but would not show himself to any enticement or challenge I could orchestrate. Thinking he was busy with a cow, I had persisted through the second and third evenings to no avail. I later found out he was entirely alone. That same moose, after a week or so, responded to my calling not by calling back, but by angrily smashing at saplings and charging me. He stopped short, fortunately, behind a thick bunch of alders, giving no opportunity for a decent rifle shot. My guide, inconveniently besides, had fled.

Anyway, I always tell people—you're not a good moose hunter unless you know something of moose tactics. The most important thing to know is that during the mating season male and female moose are rather apathetically looking for each other. Bulls are restless and somewhat aggressive. Cows are moody and cranky. A bull is polygamous, but his problem is he can't gather together a herd of cows to make the breeding of them convenient. He can only gather one cow at a time—one that is pre-estrous—and then he must stay with her until she is receptive. Afterwards he bites the bullet and moves around to find another almost-ready cow. Whitetail bucks breed whitetail does in this manner as well—but deer are more energetic and travel faster and their populations tend to be concentrated so deer reproduction proceeds efficiently. In moose habitat there aren't that many moose—stands to reason—and even though moose can be pretty fast on their feet, if necessary for short distances, they seem to be lazy and I believe they are reluctant to travel, even for breeding purposes.

Cows can be estrous two or three times during a breeding season—early September to early November. This means that Mother Nature has contrived an easement for the moose's laziness and inefficiency. A cow lets out a pleading bawl to attract bulls when she is becoming estrous. She is willing to perhaps travel a short distance. A bull, hearing her, and provided he's free of any current obligation, is likewise agreeable to a shortly distant rendezvous. This is why calling moose—the hunter with some device imitating a cow—is most effective at a range of 200 yards from where the bull is, in my opinion. The hunter is asking the bull to travel a reasonable distance.

A bull depends on the wind to carry his scent to a cow or another bull—especially a lesser bull. That is why a large bull seems always eager to get upwind of a hunter calling. (You would think it would be just the opposite—but it isn't, I assure you.) By this tactic he's saying to the supposed cow, "If you like my scent, honey, then come to me." Or he's saying to the supposed lesser bull, "You can't stink any worse than I do." During the peak of the rut, bulls urinate in muddy depressions, then roll in them. The urine of a prime bull is hormone-rich and stinks more than the urine of a lesser bull. Of course, if two actual bulls can't agree who stinks better, they fight about it. On one occasion I recall chancing upon two such great moose, quite exhausted, with antlers locked together. I sent Pierre to fetch the chainsaw and after several hours he appeared with that device and some members of his tribe—or family, because Pierre has always been vague to me about his intimate relationships. Pierre carried the chainsaw, of course, but these other individuals were toting a multitude of butchering implements and three cases of Ziploc heavy duty freezer bags.

"What took so long?" I asked.

"Got lost," Pierre responded, an anticipatory gleam in his one good eye.

"We don't need all these people, Pierre."

"Moose not dead yet?"

"They take turns vibrating every minute or so."

"We go. Come back later. Unless you shoot?"

"Oh, no! No! Hardly sporting, Pierre."

"You can't miss. Point rifle. Close eyes. Pull trigger. But maybe you forget bullets."

"No, Pierre. I want you to chainsaw the bulls apart."

"Make big mess. How?"

"Cut one horn off that one." I pointed. "Cut two horns off the other." I redirected my finger. "And then cut the only horn remaining."

"Better I cut horns of one bull only."

"No."

"What we do when both bulls have no horns? We give them cookies?"

"Just do it! Do it!"

Pierre started the chainsaw. His relatives retreated to the canoes, jumping in. Each seemed to find a beaver-tail paddle immediately. Pierre moved toward the moose, the chainsaw sputtering and smoking. Both bulls regarded his approach with widening eyes and when the chain commenced its buzz-like cutting, the bulls began to bellow. They were quite terrified, of course. (Must have seen that horror movie!) The bull that was completely hornless first, realizing he was lightheaded, stood up first, backed away a few strides until his rear legs were in the water and then he charged at me. Fortunately my rifle, a 280 customized by Griffin & Howe in New York, was loaded, and I fired a warning shot over the back of the advancing beast. He pulled up short, coughing and sneezing—apparently he had got some antler dust up his nose. Meanwhile the other bull, still on the ground, was shaking his head about and managing thereby to save his remaining antler from the increasingly tentative thrusts of the chainsaw. When Pierre realized that the situation was becoming unmanageable, as far as he was concerned, he gingerly placed the still functioning and smoking machine on a rock, and made a dash to the nearest canoe. The others aboard received him well and in an excited fashion they launched themselves. "Shoot that one!" Pierre yelled to me, pointing a paddle at the designated moose.

"Not sporting!" I yelled back. In any case, this moose with one antler soon regained his four feet, looked about, and charged at his bald-headed brother. I fired once more with my G&H—a little low, because I think I saw some hair fly off one moose's back. No harm done, however, because both moose immediately turned and ran into the lake and commenced to swim together to the other shore.

I thought to myself—nice going, those two will still be good trophies next year for some lucky hunters.

I will only kill a moose that has been called up—and that has been called up by me personally. Otherwise I do not consider the situation sporting. To be a successful moose-caller—and I am actually—you must keep in mind that both sexes call during the mating season, but that cows call more than bulls. The bull mostly advertises his availability by his scent. The cow does so mostly by her calling. It is a biological fact, also, that moose of the Northeast Wilderness are more vocal than moose of, say, Alaska and Sweden. The reason for this is evolutionary. Visibility is very limited in the northeastern temperate forest. Cows have needed to call more in this kind of habitat to attract attention. Also, I might add, bulls have needed to stink more. Actually moose have a sharper sense of smell than whitetail deer. Unlike deer, however, they do not as readily use this ability to defend themselves. As for the moose's sense of hearing, it is also more acute, of course. Still-hunting for moose is extremely difficult for that reason alone. To take a moose by still-hunting is mostly a matter of luck. Calling must be the only practical way—and most sporting way.

The basic moose call to practice, and use proficiently, is the one beginning as a bellow and ending as a cough—the pre-estrous call. Say MOO . . . AGH to yourself several times and you're starting to get it. To understand the MOO . . . AGH better, do the following: pound or drill a hole in the center-bottom of a topless #10 (i.e., approximately quart-size) tin; secure a 40" athletic shoelace, by means of a knot at one end, through the hole; wet the shoelace; while cradling the tin against your chest, with a thumb and a forefinger pull down the length of the string. The vibrating sound produced is quite similar to MOO . . . AGH, but might sound tinny and false to the keen ears of a smart bull if the string isn't exactly wet enough or the tin not properly cradled. In any case, the tin call gives you a better idea of the natural, pre-estrous MOO . . . AGH a smart bull wants to hear.

The traditional moose-calling device is a simple megaphone. It's the best, too. No mouthpiece or reed involved as with duck, elk, and some turkey-calling devices. My device is of birchbark laced together by thongs made of spruce roots. But moose hide as a lacing works just as well. The birchbark must be pliable, of course. The bark from very old trees is much too stiff. The megaphone can be any convenient size you want it to be. The small end, however, shouldn't be so large that you can't cover it with your mouth.

Because a bull might be close by, the initial megaphoned MOO . . . AGH should be fairly soft. In fact, soft-calling is always better. You're less apt to be off-tone that way. The same principle applies in turkey-calling situations—the average tom turkey and the average bull moose can hear acutely well.

You should make three or four soft calls and then wait 15 or 20 minutes before calling again, and perhaps a little louder this time. Be alert, of course. There is nothing quite so embarrassing as calling softly, going to sleep, then calling again and discovering a bull standing ten feet away to one side of you, his ears pointed at you, his nose twitching, and his red eyes indicating outrage.

Calling too much will frighten a bull or make him suspicious. If you can hear a bull moving restlessly at a distance, keep him interested with a single soft call now and then and splash the water with your canoe paddle. For this purpose, a paddle made of cedar or maple is better than a beaver-tail affair. In this instance you want to imitate a cow moving restlessly. You may even want to fill your hat with water and then pour the water out, imitating a urinating cow. If the bull you are aware of does not show himself after this trick, then something is wrong or the bull is busy with an actual cow.

Assuming he is with a cow, and he answers your call by calling himself—telling you to be patient a few days, if possible—then what you have to do is call like an interloping, threatening bull. The series of sounds that make up this call is more complicated than MOO . . . AGH.

HOO . . . HOO . . . HOWAH . . . OOUUFF is the first part. The last sound of this is a cough. RUPPH . . . RUPPH . . . is the second part. These sounds are grunts. Both parts may be used in combination or separately. The first is actually a bull answering a pre-estrous cow and the second is a bull challenging another bull.

But you won't learn how to call moose by reading about it here. I suggest you get personal instruction from someone who knows. Other than that, the best way is to buy an instruction tape. Instruction tapes on moose calling are available through L.L. Bean, or you may write me for a tape: Norm Jolliffe, Box 680, Brooks, ME 04921, USA. Enclose a check or money order for $10. Or you may use your Visa or MasterCard. Specify that you want my moose-calling tape, because I also have tapes on hunting deer, hunting bear, and turkey-calling.

Now, getting back to that red-eyed moose standing ten feet away. Well, as soon as I was aware of his presence, I thought to myself—if this moose hunting is a real game like football, then that big fellow has just scored a touchdown. Looking at it another way . . .

CHAPTER 23

*I feel that I may not have seriously enough provided sufficient
information as to what the hunter should do after his arrow has
been released—or his bullet fired—at a moose. In any case, such
would be an appropriate way to end this manuscript.*

WHAT do you do after a hit? How do you search for a
wounded moose?

The above are two major questions that we may not
have directly addressed in some previous context. To answer the first question, the first thing you do after a hit is
make a judgment as to where on the moose this event has
occurred. If you have bright enough fletching, you can usually see where your arrow goes. With a bullet, however, the
particular spot where it enters the moose usually can only be
guessed at based on how the moose reacts.

If the moose falls immediately after you've pulled the
trigger then you must assume a hit damaging the spinal
column. Looking at a moose broadside, the spinal cord is
almost halfway between his front leg and his back, as it
curves down from the brain and before it curves up toward
the tail, and if you aimed your bullet for the lungs, but hit
just a little high of them, you might have severed that essential nerve. The moose is permanently paralyzed and soon
lifeless. However, if the bullet only damages one of the

spinal processes—the bone structures protecting the cord—
the moose will only be temporarily paralyzed. So when he
stands up again, you should be ready to fire another bullet.

A heart-shot, or a good hit in the lungs, may bring the
moose down immediately, but usually not. Sometimes the
moose will bolt wildly—but more often he will simply run
and then fall in 25 to 200 yards. If he bumps into trees and
rocks as you observe him after the hit, you should expect
him to fall closer to 25 than 200 yards. Moose habitat being
often rather thick, you may not be able to see your moose
fall, but you might be able to hear him fall. If you wait
awhile and do not follow him immediately, the chances are
he will not rise again. An indication of a good hit with a
bullet is a sudden reaction as if the animal has been slapped.
A paunch-hit is often signalled by the moose arching his
back. That's a bad hit, of course, and you should shoot again
immediately.

If you shoot at a motionless moose and he remains that
way, then you have missed. You should shoot again. Pick
the lung-spot on the moose and calm yourself down. Probably your aim wasn't that bad the first time. Probably what
happened was that your bullet hit a tree, a branch, or even a
twig. If you have a scope, pick an opening to shoot through.
It is very common for a rifleman to be overconfident and
believe that a second shot is not necessary. "He's standing
there," you say to yourself, "but I'm sure he must be dead
on his feet. My bullet placement was perfect." Shoot again
through a clear opening.

If the moose is still on his feet but staggering after
you've made a good hit, what you ought to do is anchor him
right there with a well-aimed bullet in his neck—and shoot
for the spinal cord. If you place that extra bullet in the

moose's shoulder area he won't go down that much faster and you will be ruining more meat than necessary. Just behind the moose's ears, if you go one ear-length down, is where the bullet approaching broadside should discover the spinal column and cord. If the moose has fallen after the first shots, but is obviously still alive, and you are able to approach him from behind without being seen or heard, then do so quickly. Place the extra bullet in his neck. Never approach a wounded moose from in front.

Sometimes after you've had a good hit on a moose he will show no signs of that hit but will simply trot off and disappear. The important thing here for you to do is not to panic and rush off after the animal. A wounded moose if he is aware of being pursued will walk for as long as his strength permits. If a wounded moose is not alarmed, however, after 100 to 150 yards he will stop and lie down. What you must do is confirm the fact of a good hit—i.e., blood and hair where the moose was standing when you shot him—and then as calmly as possible wait an hour or so. Meanwhile, you should be analyzing the situation.

Light blood with air-bubbles indicates a lung hit. Dark, brownish blood probably indicates a hit in the liver. Ordinary dark-red blood indicates a shot in some muscle—and a wounded moose that's apt to travel a good distance. If you see a lot of blood in the tracks of the moose close to where he was when you shot him, and the amount of blood gradually decreases, this indicates a shot in some muscle, too. However, if the amount of blood increases, then probably a large blood vessel has been hit—and you should be able to find that moose without great difficulty. Blood from a paunch-hit is dark red and usually mixed with stomach contents. Actually a paunch-hit leaves very little blood. Lots of hair where the moose was standing indicates a grazing shot—and if you ever find that moose he will be quite able-bodied, but perhaps cranky.

You should study the trees and bushes before and behind where the moose was standing. Determine the line of fire and walk it back. You can't see where a bullet entered a tree from the impact side, but the exit hole is easy to detect. Obviously if there is an exit hole with wood and bark splinters in a tree then you didn't hit the moose. If the bullet touched twigs before it got to the moose it probably exploded with perhaps a splinter or two entering the moose somewhere, with little effect, or the bullet keyholed, and possibly entered the moose somewhere with lessened energy and with probably no mortal effect. But in this last situation you do have a wounded moose, and you should have blood. Sometimes a bullet will go through a moose and then hit a tree. In this case there will not be an exit hole in the tree and the hole on the impact side will not be small and perfectly round—the bullet has lost energy and to some extent it has mushroomed before striking the tree.

In Sweden, the search for a wounded or distantly dead moose usually involves two people and a dog. The dog the Swedes use for this purpose is the Norwegian Elkhound, a breed going back 4,000 years to western Norway where it was particularly useful herding reindeer and cattle and defending against wolves and bears. Wolves and bears would still inspire some eagerness for the chase in this dog if indeed there were many of these left in Scandinavia, but there are very few and the survivors are protected by laws. However, the dog's hunting specialty always was and still is the moose. In this regard his sense of smell is so highly developed that he can detect a moose almost three miles away. As we have mentioned in a previous chapter, plenty of moose presently exist in Sweden.

In any case, in Sweden one person handles the leashed dog and the other person follows close behind with his rifle ready. This second fellow is not necessarily the person who wounded the moose, but more often the most experienced moose hunter available and the one who knows the area the best. The dog, the dog-handler, and the shooter move forward silently and carefully, checking the moose trails for just the right tracks. A trained dog is usually able to find the right tracks. The handler and the shooter trust the dog—even when he seems to be heading in the wrong direction. A wounded moose, if he is capable of coherent thought in spite of his injuries, often will attempt to head into the wind in order to catch some scent of the hunters. Probably he associates his sudden pain and weakness with human pursuit. If the moose has been paunched, he will almost certainly head for water. To do this is not difficult in moose habitat—swamps, ponds, and lakes are easy to find. A wounded moose is extremely alert.

Rarely in the Northeast Wilderness does anyone seem to have a good moose-tracking dog available. A leashed bear hound—a Walker, Plott, or Black & Tan—is an advantage trailing a wounded bear, of course. I have made good use of one or the other of these hounds on occasions. In fact, I'm going to switch to an all-purpose dog for this kind of work—a dachshund. It will go in my pack-basket along with my axe, meat-saw, and hoist. It will be trained to find wounded bears, deer, and moose; and being a small dog, it won't cost much to feed. In the winter I will use it rabbit hunting, and in between the various hunting seasons, my noble dachshund will bark at and chase cats for amusement.

If you can't find two experts with an expert dog to find your moose for you, the best thing to do is look for the moose yourself with three friends. Because you are the excited person who has just put a bullet or an arrow into a moose, you get the dummy-job of standing by the last drop of blood, or whatever other last-sign your moose made running off. Two of your friends act as wing-men, carefully checking the ground about ten yards each side of and parallel to the compass-heading of the blood-trail. They do this in order to discover sudden turns the moose might make. Your third friend—the one with the best eyes and capable of crawling on his hands and knees—follows the blood-trail. He does this doggedly—like a dog, in other words. He is methodical and calm. When he finds a new drop of blood, he calls you up and tells you to stand by it. You must obey him. There must be absolute order to this kind of blood-trailing. Talking must be avoided. Trail very quietly. You communicate with hand signals or soft whistles. There is nothing more alert than a wounded moose.

As you go along you should mark the trail with brightly colored tape or paper—high enough so that you can see it from a distance. Tape tends to be permanent and should be removed after the moose is found or the search for him abandoned. Paper is biodegradable and toilet paper disappears faster than anything in the woods—except a blood-trail after a rain. In addition to looking for blood, all the trailers should be alert to notice abnormal scuff marks or hoof prints that would indicate a failing or staggering moose. Of course when the quantity of blood is great and other sign is plentiful there is no need for marking the trail. Often there is confusion at the very end of a blood-trail. That's because the moose has doubled back on the trail and then staggered off to one side before going down.

When you find the moose, and he's dead, then you can start to talk and make noise and holler.

EPILOGUE

The best way to get to know any animal is to hunt him.

I AM glad that I ended my manuscript in a practical, serious manner admonishing my readers to dance happily around the body of their dead moose and to raise the cups high. There are reasons to celebrate. The first reason that I can see is that there exist plenty of moose in the Northeast Wilderness. The second reason is that ever since hunters bonked their quarry with clubs and rocks, once the beast was down, they danced and cheered—because the task was difficult, and they needed the meat. The task is still not without difficulty (more difficult with the bow and arrow, of course) and the meat is still utilized rather completely. Moose nose will never be popular with modern hunters, however. Moose butter—as you recall, made from moose marrow rendered down—will not be an item the modern housewife will want stocked in her refrigerator. Anita has been complaining for months that she is "sick and tired" of moose meat—we have so much of it in our freezer. I didn't get a deer this year, or a bear for that matter, either. I don't need the meat. That explains why when I did fling arrows at these particular items of big game, I missed . . . Pardon me . . . . I can hear Anita rolling around on the kitchen floor seized by fits of laughter.

As an avid hunter of bear and deer, I find it difficult not to feel depressed (although I try to hide that fact) when a hunter I know kills a bear. Claims to the contrary by outfitters and biologists, provincial and state game officials, and the Hermit of Blackfly Lake, I don't feel that bears in general are doing all that well in the Northeast Wilderness. This is because of drastic habitat alterations as well as hunting pressures. Once you shoot a bear, and he's lying there dead, he's gone and he won't ever be back. The bear reproduction rate is so slight, compared to deer and even to moose. Deer seem to thrive because of habitat alteration. Moose also benefit because of clear-cutting practices. Bears do not thrive because of any kind of habitat change. Bears would do best in a preservationist world. Deer do best the way the world is now—consumptive. Moose would probably do best, or at least hold their own, in a compromise world that is neither consumptive nor rigidly conservative with its resources.

Knowing the animal—bear, moose, or deer—is the important thing. Hunting the animal is exciting, but by killing him, you get to know him best of all. He lies there on the ground, his struggle to survive ended, his expression calmly serious. You tricked him. You shot him. The animal seems to speak to you—"Now," he says, "what are you going to do with your life, and the world." The dead animal passes whatever responsibility he had to the world to you. As primitive peoples rightly believed, the spirit of the dead animal hovers about the hunter.

★★★

"What time did you shoot the bear?" the dog-handler asked the hunter. This person was superb in the woods with his dog and by himself. He had the habit of not quite looking you in the eye, but just about an inch away from your eye.

"At 5:30," the hunter replied. His hair was cut strangely, I thought—everything was shaved except for a strip an inch wide and an inch high on top. The hunter was from New York City and he had confessed to me that the only things he killed were cockroaches when he walked into his kitchen at night to get something from his refrigerator.

"He probably got the liver," I said to the dog-handler. "Right over here is the arrow, and in that direction is where the string goes. So if you and the dog can follow the string, and everyone else stay back, to allow the dog to concentrate, when we get to the end of the string, the dog will have gotten the scent and will be able to follow it."

"We can't follow the scent?" the hunter asked. He was being serious.

"No. Our noses aren't that good. Besides we have no blood to see to follow at the end of the string. The bear is climbing the mountain. He'll die on top somewhere. Without the dog, we might find him in the morning. We might not. In any case, his meat will spoil if we don't find him tonight, in the dark. Walk carefully so you don't hurt yourself. It's much worse here than stepping on cockroaches."

"I think the dog has the scent," the dog-handler said, actually looking me right straight in the eye. This was his statement on the character and intelligence of the hunter.

I nodded in agreement. "The dog is getting tangled in the string," I said.

★★★

"Hey, the dog handler is shouting," the hunter said to me.

"What?" I asked. I had been dozing with my back against a tree.

"He's saying he found a bear."

"What?"

"He's found a dead bear, but he's not sure it's my bear. But I know he's being funny."

We made our tedious way across a ridge littered with boulders and large poplars torn up by their roots. A hurricane had killed the poplars.

"His guts are hanging out," the hunter said, arriving at the dead bear before I do. "The dog isn't happy."

"The dog likes bears with a little life in them," the handler explained. "Dead bears are no fun to chase."

"But he did it anyway!" The hunter exclaimed. Then he kissed the dog. But the dog still wasn't happy. Actually the dog looked bored and he yawned repeatedly. "Now what do we do?" the hunter asked.

"Oh, we just stay here a while and look at the bear," I said.

REFERENCES,
ACKNOWLEDGMENTS,
EXPLANATIONS, APOLOGIES

This is a work of non-fiction and fiction. The non-fiction should be considered neither authoritative nor scholarly—but it is the best I could come up with and contains my most accurate judgment concerning bear and moose. The fiction is based on true experiences. Indeed, some of the experiences are so true that they should not be considered fanciful in the least.

Prologue
The editor never said to me, "A book should be like a sandwich." But if I were an editor, that's what I would say. I do not own seven cats. I own four. One of them is not taxidermied—just acts that way. The Hermit of Blackfly Lake is fictional—no one like him living or dead. I never lived in Alaska—but the Hermit has. Griffin and Howe are indeed fancy custom gunsmiths. Clever fellows, too. I believe both are dead. Their business survives, however, and is flourishing.

Chapter 1
I consulted with some Passamaquoddies and Penobscots while researching this chapter. On the occasion described I met Julia Seton, co-author of THE GOSPEL OF

209

THE REDMAN. Her book was privately published years ago but is presently missing from my bookcase. In any case, many thanks for permission to reprint the poem. I read books borrowed from the Unity College Library. The overdue notice identifies these as: Hamilton NATIVE AMERICAN BOWS; Josephy INDIAN HERITAGE OF AMERICA; Bjorklund INDIANS OF NE AMERICA; Bonfanti BIOGRAPHIES AND LEGENDS; Wipple INDIANS; and Wilbur NE INDIANS.

Chapter 2
   A useful reference for this chapter was THE HISTORY AND STATUS OF THE BLACK BEAR IN MASSACHUSETTS AND ADJACENT NEW ENGLAND STATES by James E. Cardoza, published in 1976 by the Massachusetts Division of Fisheries and Wildlife. I believe the Thoreau source-quote came from that. (I borrowed the book from a biologist and had to return it some time ago.) Certainly other source-quotes are derived from Cardoza, and many of these I mangled to improve readability. Some changes are minor and other are major and mostly involve spelling and punctuation. The meanings of the original authors I maintained, I hope. Many thanks to Cardoza for permission to use his material thusly.
   Another useful reference for this chapter was HUNTING by Gunnar Brusewitz, published in 1969 by Allen & Unwin of London, translated by Walstan Wheeler from the Swedish JAKT, published in 1967 by Whalstrom & Widstrand of Stockholm. Brusewitz writes about bear and moose hunting from a Swedish and European point of view. His book is authoritative and scholarly.

Chapter 3

Biologists of Maine Fish and Wildlife read through the manuscript of this chapter—making corrections and comments. Thanks very much to Craig McLaughlin and Gerry Lavigne. To cook and eat parts cut from live, tranquilized bears has never been done, has never been considered, has never even been joked about. Sorry fellows if I may have implied otherwise in the draft of the manuscript that you read.

Ernest Seton's LIVES OF GAME ANIMALS is quoted from extensively in this chapter. The editor suggested that I use the material in these long quotes and put it in my own words, but I feel Seton is too great to mess with and his writing is as much of a part of natural history as are the creatures he talks about.

Permission to quote Ernest Seton is gratefully acknowledged.

Chapter 4

Biologists McLaughlin and Lavigne read this one, too.

Manly Hardy is a fascinating figure in the history of Maine natural history. His only writings available to me are by way of photocopies of photocopies of letters originally published in issues of FOREST AND STREAM MAGAZINE circa 1900. I have quoted from these letters in this chapter and other chapters. Hardy is worthy of a modern biography.

I've always known that bears attack tents. In the 6/26/87 issue of the *Bangor Daily News,* there is an account of one such attack at Baxter State Park on the tent of Kurt Bierig of Clinton, MA: "At around 3 a.m . . . . a bear began attacking his tent, causing it to collapse on top of him. The bear then grabbed Bierig, tent, sleeping bag and all, and headed for the woods. Bierig managed to scramble out of the tent and up a tree, where he remained for two hours before he was able to waken nearby campers. Several people were sleeping in another tent 20 feet away, Bierig told game wardens, but they did not awake during the attack and he was unable to rouse them by calling from his perch in the tree."

Chapter 5

Ron Masure is an acquaintance with many business interests in the Greenville area. Where I got lost was in Jackson, Maine.

Chapter 6

Much of this was originally published in FINS & FEATHERS MAGAZINE. Wayne Bosowicz is the most professional bear guide I have ever met.

Chapter 7

Tink Nathan, a friend and an expert on solving the problem of human scent, offered to read the manuscript of this chapter and make corrections and comments. I forgot to send it to him.

Chapter 8

PRECISION NEWS used to be the name of the magazine published by Precision Shooting Equipment, a manufacturer of archery equipment. PSE recently changed the name to NORTH AMERICAN BOWHUNTER. Anyway, my thanks to George Webber for letting me reprint his PRECISION NEWS article here.

Chapter 9

Much of this was originally published in OUTDOOR LIFE. People in Maine defended the humor, but folks elsewhere hated it and were not mollified by explanations. Soon after the piece was published, OL hired a new editor, who promptly contacted Outdoor Writers Association of America disclaiming his responsibility for Aristotle and Plato and whatever.

Chapter 10

I do enjoy working with a tape recorder. The way the story reads, with the voice of George Gray, is exactly as it speaks. Besides, in rural eastern Canada, people talk that way.

Chapter 11

Thank you, Bryce Towsley, for permission to reprint your article here.

Chapter 12

I have never hunted anything with a crossbow. The last thing that I could have hunted with a crossbow was Winston Woodchuck when he got into the garden at the beans. My outhouse is near the garden and I keep the crossbow in there cocked for action, because I can sit down and with the door open just a crack I can supervise the garden, and shoot a bolt if I have to. Now, don't you think that is smart? Well, the other morning I'm sitting there in the outhouse regarding the natural world through that crack, when I see the beans waving. The wind is making the corn bend to the south, but the beans are shaking definitely northward. So I get excited and grab the crossbow. I can't make noise and I can't stand up. I ease the crossbow around and open the door somewhat wider to improve the field of fire. That was a mistake because the door made a screech. I see Winston snap to attention there in the beans and commence to click his teeth. And then he's growling at me, you know, because he knows what I'm premeditating as I am regarding him. We have had other experiences at doing this—obviously. Anyway, Winston is down his hole before I have a chance to hunt him with a crossbow. I have never hunted anything with a crossbow.

Chapter 13
    Brusewitz's HUNTING is a reference for this chapter. The Finnish epic poem and Julius Caesar quotes are derived from Brusewitz. In my own edition of COMMON-TARIES I see no mention of moose antics—so Brusewitz quotes another Caesar. Anyway, permission to reprint from HUNTING is gratefully acknowledged.
    The book by Nicholas Denys—THE DESCRIPTION AND NATURAL HISTORY OF THE COASTS OF NORTH AMERICA—I did indeed have trouble borrowing. Arthur Spiess of the Maine State Museum helped direct me to the right library. Arthur is an archaeologist mostly concerned with Indian research in Maine and eastern Canada. I wish now I had time to ask him more questions.

Chapter 14
    Thank you Manly Hardy.

Chapter 15
    The important reference here is NORTH AMERI-CAN MOOSE by Randolph L. Peterson, published in 1955

by University of Toronto Press. Many thanks for permission to quote from this significant work.

Also, many thanks to biologist Karen Morris of Maine Fish and Wildlife for making corrections and comments on a manuscript of this chapter.

Chapter 16

Morris inspected a manuscript of this chapter. Peterson is a reference. The material by Francis Dunn is quoted from his article in MAINE FISH AND GAME MAGAZINE—Spring 1970. Thanks for permission to quote. The telemetry material is by Alan Crossley from his article in MAINE FISH AND WILDLIFE—Summer 1983. Thanks for permission to quote.

Chapter 17

Some of this was originally published in ARCHERY WORLD MAGAZINE under my penname, Clarence Greenleaf. It is excerpted here.

Chapter 18

Although Greenleaf appears as a character in this, the scene with him and the other events are all true. Sometimes you have to change names or not mention names so that people won't get mad at you.

Chapter 19

This one is mostly all true. The scene where I am eating kidneys on a skewer is exaggerated. The material on the moose tongue and testicles is partly fantasy. Moose-muzzle might be tasty, but I've never had any. Thank you, Manly Hardy, for the recipe.

Chapter 20
Thank you Denys and thank you George Gray.
Actually I have heard other versions of this moose story, but I think Gray's is the best.

Chapter 21
Thank you Rick Clowry for permission to reprint your moose story here.

Chapter 22
This story is fiction.

Chapter 23
I frequently find myself in situations where I'm tracking wounded game. This is my advice.

Epilogue
This describes how I feel about killing. Recently, after I had put a bullet hole in a groundhog that had been feeding in my garden, I dug a grave for the critter, and covered him up nicely with earth. I voiced the hope that he would fertilize the earth. Well, I returned to the grave half an hour later with the thought in mind that I should say a few more words, and guess what? The grave was empty. Seldom do animals that get killed get born again.